Burnt by the Sun

KINOfiles Film Companions
General Editor: Richard Taylor

Written for cineastes and students alike, KINOfiles are readable, authoritative, illustrated companion handbooks to the most important and interesting films to emerge from Russian cinema from its beginnings to the present. Each KINOfile investigates the production, context and reception of the film and the people who made it, and analyses the film itself and its place in Russian and World cinema. KINOfiles will also include films of the other countries that once formed part of the Soviet Union, as well as works by émigré filmmakers working in the Russian tradition.

KINOfiles form a part of KINO: The Russian Cinema Series.

BURNT BY THE SUN

BIRGIT BEUMERS

KINOfile Film Companion 3

I.B.Tauris *Publishers*
LONDON • NEW YORK

Published in 2000 by I.B.Tauris & Co Ltd
Victoria House, Bloomsbury Square, London WC1B 4DZ
175 Fifth Avenue, New York NY 10010
www.ibtauris.com

In the United States of America and in Canada distributed by
St Martins Press, 175 Fifth Avenue, New York NY 10010

ISBN 1 86064 396 5

A full CIP record for this book is available from the British Library
A full CIP record for this book is available from the Library of Congress

Library of Congress catalog card: available

Typeset in Monotype Calisto by the Midlands Book Typesetting Company,
Loughborough, Leicestershire
Printed and bound in Great Britain by MPG Books Ltd, Bodmin, Cornwall

Contents

List of Illustrations

Acknowledgements

I wish to thank the Arts Faculty Research Fund at Bristol University for their support with the research for this study. I would also like to express my thanks to Anatoli Ermilov at TriTe, Moscow, Peter Scott at Pathé Distribution, London, and the Agence Nicole Cann, Paris, for their generous help with the illustrations for this book. I am also deeply indebted to Anatoli Ermilov for patiently answering all my questions, and to my students for raising questions and for making lively comments in our discussion of the film. Finally, I should like to thank Julian Graffy, Nancy Condee, Josephine Woll and Richard Taylor for their comments.

Note on Transliteration

Transliteration from the Cyrillic to the Latin alphabet is a perennial problem for writers on Russian subjects. I have opted for a dual system: in the text I have used the Library of Congress system (without diacritics), but I have broken from this system (a) when a Russian name has a clear English version (e.g. Maria instead of Mariia, Alexander instead of Aleksandr); (b) when a Russian name has an accepted English spelling, or when Russian names are of Germanic origin (e.g. Yeltsin instead of Eltsin; Eisenstein instead of Eizenshtein); (c) when a Russian surname ends in -ii or -yi this is replaced by a single -y (e.g. Dostoevsky instead of Dostoevskii), and all Christian names end in a single -i; (d) when 'ia' or 'iu' are voiced (at the beginning of a word and when preceded by a vowel) they are rendered as 'ya' or 'yu' (e.g. Daneliya, Yuri) - with the sole addition of the name Asya to avoid confusion with the continent, Asia. In the scholarly apparatus I have adhered to the Library of Congress system (with diacritics) for the specialist.

Credits

English Title: BURNT BY THE SUN
Original Title: UTOMLENNYE SOLNTSEM
French Title: SOLEIL TROMPEUR

Director: Nikita Mikhalkov
Release: 1994 (Cannes, May 1994; Nizhnii Novgorod, 12 July 1994; Moscow 2 November 1994)
Television premiere: 18 May 1997, ORT (First Russian Television Channel)
Production: Studio TriTe (Russia), Camera One (France), Goskino (Russian State Committee for Cinema), Russian Club (Russkii Klub), Canal + (France)
Co-Production: Russia and France
Licence No 1103394 (4 April 1994), Visa d'exploitation 84.037
International Sales: Pyramide International, Claude Cheval
UK Distribution: Pathé
Video Release: VHS G8859S (Guild Home Video)
Sound Track: 'Soleil Trompeur/Burnt by the Sun', Auvidis, France, 1994 (CD K1011)
Running Time: 142 minutes (Russian); 129 minutes (English)
Frames: 1121 (Russian)
Parts: 16
Length: 4137 metres (Russian); 3697 metres (English)

Awards:
Cannes Festival 1994: Special Grand Jury Prize and Ecumenical Prize

American Academy Awards (Oscars) 1995: Best Foreign
 Language Film 1994
State Prize of the Russian Federation 1995

Cast

Dmitri (Mitia)	Oleg Menshikov
Sergei Petrovich Kotov	Nikita Mikhalkov
Marusia (Musia)	Ingeborga Dapkunaite
Nadia	Nadia Mikhalkova
Vsevolod Konstantinovich	Viacheslav Tikhonov
Katia Mokhova	Svetlana Kriuchkova
Kirik	Vladimir Ilyin
Lidia Stepanovna	Alla Kazanskaya
Elena Mikhailovna	Nina Arkhipova
Driver	Avangard Leontiev
Philippe	André Umansky
Olga Nikolaevna	Inna Ulianova
Liuba	Liubov Rudneva
NKVD Officer	Vladimir Riabov
First NKVD man	Vladimir Belousov
Second NKVD man	Alexei Pokatilov
Lieutenant	Evgeni Mironov

Based on a story by	Nikita Mikhalkov
Screenplay	Nikita Mikhalkov
	Rustam Ibragimbekov
Dialogue	Rustam Ibragimbekov
	Nikita Mikhalkov
Music	Eduard Artemiev
Director of Photography	Vilen Kaliuta
Art Directors	Vladimir Aronin
	Alexander Samulekin
Costume Designer	Natalia Ivanova
Make-up	Larisa Avdiushko
Assistant Director	Vladimir Krasinsky
Editor	Enzo Meniconi
Sound	Jean Umansky
	André Rigaut

Sound Mixer	Vincent Arnardi
	Thierry Lebon
Production Co-ordinator	Anatoli Ermilov
Executive Producer	Leonid Vereshchagin
Producers	Nikita Mikhalkov
	Michel Seydoux
Co-producers	Nicole Cann
	Jean-Louis Piel
	Vladimir Sedov
Casting	Tamara Odintsova
Line Producer	Leonid Vereshchagin
Production Manager (Paris)	Armand Barbault
Production Manager (Moscow)	Vladimir Ninov
Production Manager (Nizhnii Novgorod)	Vladimir Denisov

Music:
'Utomlennoe solntse' by Jerzy Peterburgski
Extracts from the music of Dmitri Shostakovich, Isaak Dunaevsky, Alexander Tsfasman, V. Trofimov, S. Dezhkin, Yuli Khait with lyrics by Boris Kornilov, Vasili Lebedev-Kumach, V. Shmitgof, Pavel German, I. Alvek
Music performed by the State Film Symphony Orchestra, Conductor Sergei Skripka
Instrumental Quartet: Mark Simkin, Efim Vyshkin, Alexander Bashlatov, Viktor Agapov

Filmed on location in Moscow, dacha interior in Nizhnii Novgorod, and village scenes in and around Nikolina Gora, between 19 July and 17 November 1993.

Budget:
$3.6 million

Introduction

When I first saw *Burnt by the Sun* in 1994 I thought that, with its perfected shots and rounded plot, it resembled too much the Hollywood-style films with their neat narratives that pose no questions and make everything only too clear; the sort of film that would impress the Academy. Indeed, the film went on to win the top Hollywood award, the Oscar (Academy Award) for the Best Foreign Language Film.

Beyond the neatly polished surface I gradually discovered a host of references to the events and culture of the 1930s; every gesture, every turn of phrase, every tune had a broader significance, within the film and beyond it. The complexity of the motives which made the main characters act as they did is as ambiguous as is the final cut of the film. Questions such as 'who is the victim' and 'who is the victimizer' are carefully held in suspension throughout the film. In the process of analysis I came to regard the film highly for making a very complex system of references and signs seem so simple, as if naturally flowing from the cutting board of a director who must be very talented to delude the spectator with his 'nice little story'.

Who, then, is this talented director who makes headlines not only with his films? How did he manage to make a film that could win an Oscar at a time when the Russian film industry was in crisis?

Mikhalkov, Film-maker and Public Figure

Nikita Sergeevich Mikhalkov (b. 1945) is the son of Sergei Mikhalkov, a writer of children's stories, plays and the text of the Soviet state anthem (1943). His mother, Natalia Konchalovskaya, was a poet from an aristocratic background. Mikhalkov's elder brother, Andrei (Mikhalkov)-Konchalovsky (b. 1937), is also a film-maker. Konchalovsky's films include *Asya's Happiness* [Asino schast'e, aka Istoriia Asi

Kliachinoi, kotoraia liubila da ne vyshla zamuzh, 1967, rel. 1988], the two adaptations of the nineteenth-century classics *A Nest of Gentlefolk* based on Ivan Turgenev [Dvorianskoe gnezdo, 1969] and *Uncle Vanya* [Diadia Vania, 1971], based on Anton Chekhov's play, and the epic *Siberiade* [1979] before he left for Hollywood in the 1980s, and successfully continued in film-making with *Maria's Lovers* [1984], *Runaway Train* [1985], and *Tango & Cash* [1989]. Since the early 1990s he has been working both in Russia and abroad: *The Inner Circle* [Blizhnii krug, Russia/Italy, 1991], *The Little Speckled Hen* [Kurochka Riaba, Russia, 1994], *The Odyssey* [USA, 1996].

Nikita Mikhalkov began his career as an actor in the 1960s before completing his studies as a film director. In 1974 he made his first feature, *At Home among Strangers, a Stranger at Home* [Svoi sredi chuzhikh, chuzhoi sredi svoikh], followed by *A Slave of Love* [Raba liubvi, 1975], *Unfinished Piece for a Mechanical Piano* [Neokonchennaia p'esa dlia mekhanicheskogo pianino, 1977]; *Five Evenings* [Piat' vecherov, 1978], *Oblomov* [1979], *Kinfolk* [Rodnia, 1981] and *A Private Conversation* [Bez svidetelei, 1983]. He has since attained international renown with the Italian co-productions *Dark Eyes* [Ochi chernye, 1987] and *Autostop* [1990], and the French co-productions *Urga* [1991], which won the Golden Lion at the Venice Film Festival in 1991 and an Oscar nomination in 1993, and *Burnt by the Sun* [1994] which won the Grand Prix at the Cannes Film Festival in 1994 and an Oscar award for Best Foreign Language Film in 1995.

Apart from being a very talented actor and a film-maker of international standing, Mikhalkov also occupies several influential positions in Russian cultural politics: in 1990 he became adviser to the then prime minister on cultural issues; in 1991 he joined the UNESCO Commission for Culture; and in 1993 he was elected president of the Russian Fund for Culture. He stood for election to parliament in the government party 'Our Home is Russia', winning a seat that he later declined. Since 1989 he has run his own production company, TriTe (Three T's, which abbreviate the company's motto 'Trud, Tovarishchestvo, Tvorchestvo', or 'Work, Camaraderie, Creativity'). The company has a publishing arm called 'Russian Archive' that has published documents relating to Russian history.

In December 1997 Mikhalkov was elected chairman of the Filmmakers' Union. His election was a vote of trust: he initially carried out an audit of the Union properties before he presented his programme and called for an extraordinary congress for all the Union members to approve his new direction. Mikhalkov was the only figure who could, by his charisma alone, inspire trust and confidence, and who had enough political clout to rescue the dilapidated homes for veteran film-makers from ruin or sale. Five months later, in his speech to the Fourth (Extraordinary) Congress of the Film-makers' Union in May 1998, Mikhalkov proposed the creation of an extra-budgetary fund to support the film industry, to be made up from fees collected from licensing video retail. The funds would be invested in the reconstruction of cinemas, the production of new films and the renovation and maintenance of the Union's properties. Mikhalkov thereby attempted to transfer to the Union certain functions presently still carried out by the State Department for Cinematography (Goskino). Furthermore, he argued very strongly that film-makers should instil hope in the cinema audience, and he dwelt on the need to recreate the myth of a Russian national hero in order to regain a spirit of patriotism that had bonded the Soviet Union in the past, and that bonds America now. According to Mikhalkov, Russian cinema should project a national identity, and inspire the people to believe in Russia's future. His view that Russian cinema needs positive heroes (despite its potentially dangerous echoes of the Socialist Realist slogans of the 1930s calling for a 'varnished', fairy-tale reality) is a perceptive assessment of the state of contemporary cinema, which – like contemporary politics – lacks direction.

However, any attempt to give direction and channel energies requires leadership and authority. This is what Mikhalkov has assumed both in his new role in the Film-makers' Union and with his latest film, *The Barber of Siberia* [Sibirskii tsiriul'nik, 1998]. This film is, with a $45 million budget, one of the most expensive feature films ever made outside Hollywood; with two-thirds of the dialogue in English, this romantic love story with star actors from Russia and Europe should fare well in international sales. Only a man of Mikhalkov's reputation could have secured a third of the film's funding from the Russian government, while his successful collaboration with one of France's most powerful producers, Michel Seydoux (Camera One), secured him a French partner for the project who could raise the remainder of the funding.

Yet Mikhalkov's attempts to set an example for film production and release, to show Russian film-makers how to make a good film, and to set moral guidelines embodied in the characters of his film, have been met with envy, even hostility, by the Russian press. Moreover, part of the media hype around Mikhalkov was generated by his evasive statements as to whether he would stand in the next presidential elections. He has explained in several interviews that he would consider standing for president if he felt that the people wanted him to do so, but that it was premature to make a decision at present.

In *The Barber of Siberia* Mikhalkov idealizes the pre-Revolutionary past and the figure of the tsar as the father of all Russians. He cast himself in the role of Tsar Alexander III, a reactionary and nationalist ruler who insisted on the conversion of all Russians to Orthodoxy, which he perceived as the ideal form for the preservation of moral values and the discipline necessary for his autocratic rule. Such a portrayal is significant both in the context of Mikhalkov's political 'ambitions' and in light of the absence of a father-figure in so many contemporary Russian films of the post-Soviet period, when soldiers no longer know what they are fighting and dying for (as, for example, in Sergei Bodrov's *The Prisoner of the Mountains* [Kavkazskii plennik, 1996]).

Russian Cinema in the 1990s

Since the collapse of the Soviet Union in 1991 Russian films have almost vanished from the repertoire of Russian cinemas because of problems with distribution; even less prominent is their presence in international sales: Sokurov's *Mother and Son* [Mat' i syn, 1997], Bodrov's *Prisoner of the Mountains*, Chukhrai's *The Thief* [Vor, 1997] are the principal exceptions. Russian post-Soviet films show a concern with the loss of values in a society that is more and more consumer-orientated and materialistic; they offer a picture of a bleak reality, and no future. This explains why they are shunned by Russian audiences and international sales agents alike. Yet why do contemporary film-makers indulge in such a negative portrayal of life in Russia?

After the demise of communism, film-makers rejected above all the demand to construct the future. Instead, they began to portray the reality that surrounded them without the ideological constraints (beautifying, varnishing, showing the 'bright future') hitherto imposed. What they saw was a grim picture: beggars on the streets, impoverished pensioners, economic chaos, street crime, Mafia-ordered shootings, pornographic magazines and videos, decaying houses and ramshackle communal apartments, and the emergence of a new class, the 'New Russians', who adapted quickly and learnt how to make money in a society under reconstruction. Literature, film, visual arts and music that reflect this bleak reality are commonly referred to as *chernukha* (literally: that which is made black).

The mainstream of Russian cinema indeed indulges in this blackness, or bleakness, and offers neither alternative nor perspective. Filmmakers have rejected their 'mission' to act as prophets (a mission taken on by many film-makers of the Soviet period), or to guide morally and aesthetically. The audience, in turn, have rejected films which offer no positive outlook or spiritual guidance amid the chaos, and have turned instead to Latin American soap operas screened daily on Russian television.

The Soviet film industry had been nationalized after the Revolution, and as such it had always relied on the state to finance and distribute films. The film studios would act as producer, employ directors, actors and technical personnel, provide all the facilities for making the film, and take charge of distribution. The audience was important, but not crucial in the funding of a film. This system of production collapsed with the demise of the Soviet state. What remained were large, unmanageable studios, which were gradually split up into small, independent production companies; a State Department for Cinematography (Goskino) with an annual budget to help the national cinema; and a huge number of large, uncomfortable cinemas.

As the infrastructure was crumbling, it became clear that the function of cinema had to change with a changing social model. The Soviet state had built huge cinemas that needed to be refurbished and modernized, converted into multiplexes and fitted with Dolby systems. The old cinemas attracted fewer and fewer people. Screenings dropped by half; numerous cinemas were closed, while a few were refurbished and others newly built. In 1998 some six cinemas were operating on a profitable basis. Television also deflected audiences away from cinema, and the video market made any film available for the price of a cinema ticket or less. Video piracy poses a huge problem to the film industry, since most films are copied illegally so that there is no reliable return for the film industry from video sales.

This collapse of the market led to a dramatic crisis in the film industry. During the first post-Soviet years the film industry was used to launder money, and large investments were made which enabled film-makers to produce whatever they wanted irrespective of public demand. The number of films produced doubled, while fewer films were distributed nationally and internationally. Once the film industry's laundering function had been brought to a halt by new legislation, film-makers lost their sense of the audience and relied on state funding; in the period after 1994 film production plummeted. Since 1997 film production has picked up again, and independent production companies have produced some successful films, targeted at specific audiences.

But catering for an audience, making a film for the masses, remains a derogatory term for Russian film-makers and critics alike. These two professions identify themselves with the intelligentsia, which prefers films made for the intellectual elite, the so-called *auteur* cinema (*avtorskoe kino*), while they frown upon anything that even sounds accessible to the masses. Thus, as long as the state has no law in place that would offer tax incentives to investors, the cinema relies on the state for funding, and therefore remains self-centred, seeking no contact with the audience, and does not aim to cater for the masses, or to entertain and serve a commercial goal. Yet while the cinema remains exclusively self-centred, investors will not be interested in an industry that offers not the slightest chance of return. The divide between art-film and commercially oriented film production could not be greater.

In this divide, Mikhalkov, aware of audience taste, stands on the 'commercially orientated' side. Although he himself comes from the Soviet intelligentsia, his films speak to a general audience rather than the select few. This is why he is loved by Russian audiences, and hated by the liberal intelligentsia; why he has received international acclaim for his films, and why *Burnt by the Sun* – his best film, in the opinion of critics, supporters, and the American Film Academy – deserves a study of this kind.

1. Plot Synopsis and Summary

Synopsis

On a Sunday in June 1936 the secret service (NKVD) officer Mitia accepts and carries out a special assignment: the arrest of the Red Army Commander Kotov at his family's dacha near Moscow. Meanwhile, Kotov enjoys domestic happiness with his wife Marusia and daughter Nadia. Mitia, a friend of the family and Marusia's first love, arrives and spends the day with the family, taking Kotov back to Moscow with him in the evening. Upon his return to Moscow Mitia succeeds in his second suicide attempt (having tried to shoot himself the day before): he cuts his wrists in the bath.

Summary

In the early hours of the morning a black limousine drops Mitia by the entrance to an apartment block on the embankment of the Moscow river. He enters the building and goes to his flat, where his French tutor Philippe awaits him. The phone rings, but neither Mitia nor Philippe picks it up for a long time. Instead, Mitia sits in an armchair and plays 'Russian roulette' with his revolver: he holds it against his temple and fires, but he pulls the trigger on an empty cartridge. Philippe reads out to him a newspaper article about fireballs striking down anything that moves, while Mitia corrects his Russian. Eventually, Mitia picks up the phone and agrees to take on an assignment.

The film titles are set against the background of a quartet playing the 1930s tango 'Utomlennoe solntse' [The Weary Sun]. The band

1. Kotov (Nikita Mikhalkov), Nadia (Nadia Mikhalkova) and Marusia
(Ingeborga Dapkunaite) as a happy family

*contrasts-
first scene-
sad → happy*

performs at a dance pavilion in a park on a cold winter's day. A couple,
Kotov and Marusia, dance while a little girl (Nadia) is sitting on a
bench.

*reminds-
Stalin =
paranoid*

Months later. It is summer in the countryside and children are
playing in the fields when tanks are seen approaching. Commander
Kotov is enjoying his day off in the bathhouse (*bania*), where his
daughter Nadia is sitting on his back lashing him with birch twigs.

A horseman rides towards the dacha and passes a truck with furniture whose driver is asking for directions. The horseman is in a hurry
to find Kotov and, although the maid Mokhova tells him Kotov is not
to be disturbed, he finds the commander in the bathhouse and asks
him to help: the harvest is being crushed by tanks conducting a
manoeuvre. Kotov initially chases the man away, telling him to find
the village chairman and not to disturb him on a Sunday, but he
eventually agrees to help: he mounts a horse and rides off. When
Kotov arrives in the fields he speaks with the lieutenant who does not
recognize him: Kotov borrows a cap and poses in profile – his portraits
are displayed everywhere in universities, schools, assembly halls – and
the lieutenant immediately succumbs to his orders. Kotov phones the

commanding officer and orders him to reorganize the manoeuvre while the aeroplanes are already flying across the field.

Back at the dacha Marusia's family (her mother, grandmother and uncle, her grandmother's friend Elena with her son Kirik) gather for breakfast. During breakfast the family talk about the past while Mokhova cries in her room, because the two old ladies have thrown *→ theme* away her medicine to which she had become addicted.

Meanwhile, Liuba (the uncle's colleague from the Faculty of History), walks through the village; the truck with the furniture stops and the driver asks her the way to the village of Zagorianka, which she does not know. Kirik rides past them on a bike and confirms Liuba's assertion that this is the village of KhLAM, the village of 'Artists, Writers, Painters and Musicians'.

Kirik arrives at the dacha and plays a record of 'The Weary Sun'. All those present indulge in memories of the past, and compare themselves to characters in a Chekhov play. Nadia sings, grimaces and *naïve to* mocks Kirik who is chasing after women, drinks too much and *meaning.* borrows money.

At a construction site men are seen to be working on a hot-air balloon (dirigible). *→ unseen, what is it?, tension.*

Kirik flirts with Liuba. Mokhova fishes for her pills while Nadia watches and pities her. The old ladies rest inside the house, trying on a coat and puzzling about the nature of the holiday (Day of Dirigibles and Aeronautics). *→ they are Tsarists*

Pioneers are marching along the street to the sounds of Soviet music, and carrying a portrait of Stalin. Nadia stands by the gate and watches *→ Stalin* them with a longing to join them. At the end of the parade comes a bearded old man in a raincoat, with a trumpet, sunglasses and a cane; he appears to be blind. He approaches the gate and praises Nadia as a good girl who will soon be a pioneer (member of the communist children's organization). He introduces himself as a magician from the Maghreb, but he might also be a doctor who could help the maid, so Nadia asks him in. Once in the house, he starts acting the fool and everybody gathers around him to find out who he is. He sits at the piano, playing and singing; the family recognize the family friend Mitia as he takes off his disguise. Eventually, Marusia introduces him to Kotov, whom he already knows.

Mitia asks for some water and goes to wash his face. Marusia's mother learns from Mitia that he is a musician and is married with three children. The family gathers at the table for coffee, but there is a tension between the former lovers Marusia and Mitia, and between the 'rivals' Kotov and Mitia. Kotov suggests they go for a swim.

The party sets off to the beach on the banks of a river. Loud music is played from amplifiers to celebrate the Day of Dirigibles and Aeronautics. Nadia watches the pioneers swim in the river: she wants to be a pioneer, too, and to follow orders indicated by the instructor's whistle. Kotov takes Nadia for a ride in a boat while Mitia and Marusia stay at the beach. Kotov explains to Nadia that the future holds a wonderful life for her in the new Soviet land that he is helping to build. Mitia learns that Marusia tried to cut her wrists when he left her ten years ago. An evacuation exercise begins, and Marusia leaps up to go for a swim; Mitia, with his clothes on, runs into the water and takes a long dive. Marusia and Mitia get out of the water at the place where Mitia found her when she had once run away from home. Only 16 at the time, she had discovered that her mother had started an affair with Kirik only a month after her father's death. Mitia is amazed to find life at the dacha unchanged, only without him: he has been obliterated from that life. During a gas-attack evacuation practice everybody is asked to put on gas masks. Marusia and Mitia pretend to be injured in order to be taken away on a stretcher.

Kotov and Nadia return only to find that everyone has gone. Kotov hurries back home and finds Mitia's clothes hanging on the line. He runs into the house where he finds Marusia and Mitia, both wearing the gas masks, playing the cancan on the piano. Gradually, everybody joins in Marusia's dance while Kotov stands aside. He then sits at the table to start lunch: he cannot speak French like the others in the room do, and therefore claims to have been unable to invite them to join him at the table.

The truck driver stops at the construction site and is chased away: he still cannot find Zagorianka.

At the dacha, people reminisce about the past and sing arias. Mitia tells Nadia a fairy tale: a boy named Yatim was adopted by the magician Sirob, who had a daughter, Yasum. They led a happy life, which ended abruptly because of the war. Yatim had to go to the front and then abroad. He was away for ten years, always remembering his happy home. When he returned his parents had died, and he found that Yasum had grown up into a beautiful girl. Nadia claims to know the end of the story: Yatim and Yasum will marry and live happily ever after. Yet Mitia disappoints her: an important man whose name he cannot remember sent him away and married Yasum. As he tells the story, a fireball passes over the wood, gradually approaching the house and entering the room, making the glass of a picture burst before it leaves through the window and travels away over the woods, burning one single tree to the ground.

Mitia takes the guitar and plays 'The Weary Sun'. Marusia runs upstairs and is followed by Kotov, who overpowers her with his affection and they make love. Kotov then admits that he sent Mitia away ten years ago. But for Kotov, there was always a choice: while Mitia could have refused to leave the country (although he would then have been arrested and executed), Kotov himself would leave his family for love of his country, not for fear of losing his life, as Mitia did.

Mitia admits to Kirik that he is not married, but serves in the NKVD. Kirik tells Mitia that Marusia tried to kill herself when he left. Mitia teaches Nadia to tap dance and competes with her to see who can hold a note longer. Nadia is enthusiastic when she hears that he will be picked up by a car. He then briefs Kotov that he has come to arrest him, yet Kotov asks him not to tell anyone and suggests they play football.

The truck driver is still looking for the delivery address, but is now in a field where he is chased away by a peasant.

Everybody plays football in a clearing in the woods. When the ball goes astray in the woods, Kotov looks for it and is followed by Mitia who reminds him of his impending arrest. Kotov challenges the past as told by Mitia in the story: Mitia forgot to say that, in 1923, he became a secret agent of the OGPU (the secret service from 1922 to 1934) and denounced eight White officers. Mitia argues that he was forced to do this. Kotov interprets Mitia's threat to arrest him as personal revenge, when Mitia threatens Kotov: he will soon be made to confess to conspiracy, and if he will not sign the required confession, the secret service will remind him of his wife and child. Kotov hits Mitia in the face, and when Nadia comes looking for her father Mitia pretends that nothing has happened and surfaces with the ball. The pioneers come to congratulate Kotov on the holiday.

Kotov gets ready to leave, putting on his uniform. A black limousine arrives, observed by Nadia from behind the gate; then she leaves the garden to look closely at the car and speak to the three men who are munching food. Nadia tells Kotov to hurry up since Mitia has promised that she may sit at the wheel and go for a ride with them to the end of the village.

They all go to the gate to see Kotov and Mitia off. Nadia sits at the wheel with Kotov and Mitia at the back. The car drives off, and stops after a while for Nadia to get out and run back home through the fields as she hums 'The Weary Sun'.

The car drives on and Kotov proposes a drink to the holiday and a song. He is convinced that he will be able to sort out the misunderstanding of his arrest by calling Stalin on his direct line. The truck is blocking the road; the driver is still seeking Zagorianka. The driver recognizes Kotov, and, as the latter wants to tell him the way, he is held back in the car and beaten up; the truck driver, witnessing the scene, is shot by one of the officers. Mitia is about to light a cigarette when the dirigible balloon with Stalin's portrait rises. Mitia salutes Stalin with a cynical grin on his face. Back in the car Mitia looks at the weeping Kotov.

The next morning Mitia is back in his Moscow flat. He is lying in the bath whistling 'The Weary Sun' as a fireball emerges from outside, entering through the window, crossing over the piano, and leaving again through the window, which reveals a view looking out on to the red stars of the Kremlin towers. The phone is ringing while the bath water turns red with the blood flowing from Mitia's slashed wrists.

The titles complete the narrative: Kotov, Sergei Petrovich, commander of the Red Army, was shot on 12 August 1936; he was posthumously rehabilitated on 27 November 1956. Kotova, Maria Borisovna was sentenced to 10 years in a prison camp and died there in 1940; she was posthumously rehabilitated on 27 November 1956. Nadia Kotova was arrested with her mother on 12 June 1936 and fully rehabilitated on 27 November 1956. She now lives in Kazakhstan, where she works in a music school.

The film is dedicated to those 'burnt by the sun of the revolution'.

2. The Film in Frames

The English and Russian Versions

The English version differs from the Russian original in a number of places. The Russian version is 13 minutes longer than the English subtitled print released on video (142 and 129 minutes).

Broadly speaking, the following cuts have been made: before Mitia's departure in the black limousine from the dacha everybody gathers by the gate and Mitia, who is carrying a guitar in both versions, comments that they have not sung all day. He conducts the women singing 'Evening Bells', then says farewell to Marusia, and gets into the car which drives off as the women continue the song. This sequence is omitted in the English print. Another detail is the omission of a remark Marusia makes about Mitia's scar on his shoulder. Her concern for him in the conversation before the swim casts a different light on the relationship between them: Marusia actually cares for Mitia. Overall, chunks of the dialogues during dinner have been omitted, largely concerning the new regime and recollections of the times gone by.

The cuts omit the least relevant episodes and those sequences that are unfamiliar to the immediate cultural context of a Western audience. The song 'Evening Bells' has little meaning in a non-Russian context, and some of the conversation relating to the purges among university staff would be equally difficult to comprehend for a non-specialist audience.

The table of dialogue, image and sound in the sequences of the film is based on the Russian version and gives those sections omitted in the English version in square brackets.

The Original Scenario and the Film

In the original scenario published in the Russian journal *Kinostsenarii* [Filmscripts], no. 4 (1994) a clock strikes in the first scene at Mitia's flat to indicate the time, while there is no radio. Philippe reads the different newspaper reports about the show trials, which in the film are transmitted by radio. Instead of the radio, Mitia listens to Puccini's *Madame Butterfly*, whilst in the film an aria from the opera is sung by Elena Mikhailovna at the dacha. The radio that features in the film gives additional emphasis to the centrality and dominance of Moscow: there are a telephone, a car and a radio as well as newspapers, and thus all the sources of communication are to hand in the capital. At the dacha, there are no radio and telephone, and perhaps not even any electricity.

In the scenario Mitia has a slight scar on his forehead, and a large scar on his shoulder. This shows that he has fought in the war and endured physical suffering. The omission of the reference to the scar on his shoulder in the English version eliminates any physical evidence of his story about his participation in the war.

The fireball hits moving objects and people, according to the report in the papers, and also those who run away from it. In the scenario Mitia spots the fireball at the dacha, warns of the danger, and leads the fireball out into the street when it poses a threat to Kirik. In this version he is even more of a 'missionary' ready to put his own life at risk for the safety of Marusia's family.

The scenario stipulates that the medicines are thrown into the fire, rather than into the river. Yet fire and the colour red in the film are reserved for actions with political significance. The water imagery is generally less rigidly developed in the scenario, in which Mitia does not wash his face for a second time at the dacha, and Kotov and Nadia swim in the river.

The scenario also included an episode with a Georgian man who wants to cut across the estate in order to get to his destination more quickly. He too, like the driver, is on his way, yet he knows where he is going. A minor and peripheral episode repeating a theme elaborated elsewhere, this was omitted altogether in the film.

Marusia is even more determined that she 'belongs' to Kotov: after they make love, she believes she has conceived a boy, and she actively encourages Kotov to send Mitia away.

Finally, the scenario concluded with Nadia sitting on the Arbat, a pedestrian zone in central Moscow, now an old woman, playing the accordion and collecting money. A flashback would show her sitting on the bench in the park as a little girl, while the dance floor where her parents once tangoed is empty. This sequence would have closed another structural circle of the film, whose first frames in Moscow are followed by the couple dancing in the snow-covered pavilion: the film would have moved back both to Moscow, and to the pavilion.

2. Nadia as an old woman on the Arbat (a scene not featured in the film)

3. The pavilion where the Kotovs dance the tango

The differences between the scenario and the film largely affect the imagery, which is treated with more consistency in the film, and some episodes that would have diverged from the main line of the narrative or would have made the plot more explicit (Nadia on the Arbat, Marusia having conceived a child, the theme of directions lost or found).

Structure

In terms of its content the film could be divided into five acts, which would follow the classical structure of tragedy: (1) exposition, consisting of contrasts: Moscow and the countryside; summer and winter; the suicidal Mitia and the life-giving couple with a child; (2) potential conflict: Kotov the powerful military man and Kotov at the dacha with his wife's intellectual family; (3) the central conflict: the past returns with Mitia, while a temporary escape is provided by the swimming; (4) escalation of the conflict: Mitia implicates Kotov in the fairy tale and announces his arrest; (5) catastrophe: destruction (Kotov, the truck-driver, the family) and self-destruction (Mitia).

This section will provide a detailed description of the dialogue, imagery and sound, and offer a commentary for each part of the film. For this purpose, the division of the film into 16 parts in Mikhalkov's dialogue sheets has been adopted.

1 Dialogue	Image	Sound/Music	Commentary
	A close-up of a red star on a Kremlin tower widens into a panorama shot of the Stone Bridge decorated with red flags; its railings and the steps of the underpath are being cleaned with a hose. A black car drives across the bridge and stops in front of a grey house (the House on the Embankment), decorated with a red banner.	diegetic: bells from the Kremlin tower strike 6 a.m.; steps of soldiers marching on bridge; water hose; engine of car.	The black limousine and the house where Mitia lives indicate that he belongs to the upper Party apparatus (nomenklatura). Moscow is presented as the centre of Soviet power: red flags, red stars, red banners.
	Mitia gets out of the car, enters the house, ascends in the lift and opens the door to his flat.	diegetic: noise of lift	
Philippe complains in French how late Mitia is: it is six o'clock.	Philippe opens the door from inside, looks at his watch. Mitia takes off his coat and hat, then throws his jacket to Philippe.		
Mitia tells Philippe to speak Russian. Philippe had been hired in 1901 to teach Mitia French. Mitia asks Philippe to turn the lights off and switch the radio on.	Mitia goes into the bathroom to wash his face, as the camera closes up on his shaving knife.	diegetic: radio transmission of the end of a speech by chief prosecutor Vyshinsky; time: 6.15 a.m.	The camera closes up on the shaving knife, the instrument with which Mitia will eventually kill himself. The speech of the chief prosecutor Vyshinsky anticipates the show trials of 1936–38.

The phone has been ringing all day. Philippe reads out an article about fireballs hitting objects and people in motion while Mitia corrects his Russian pronunciation.	Mitia goes into the living room and sits by the phone. First he plays with a cigarette, then with a revolver. Philippe sits in another chair with the newspaper; the clock on the table shows the time: 6.15 a.m. Mitia takes the bullets out of the pistol, then puts them all on the table next to the ashtray. He places one bullet back into the cartridge, holds the pistol to his temple and pulls the trigger: no shot is fired.	diegetic: phone rings diegetic: Soviet march music on the radio diegetic: radio announcement of a concert requested by the peasant workers	A lot of dialogue is offscreen: Philippe and Mitia appear not to speak to each other. This reflects the concern with sound and appearance rather than content in Mitia's correction of Philippe's Russian. The article suggests that the fireball is part of the activities and political conspiracy directed against Stalin. The fireball is thus linked to Mitia's fate. Philippe takes no notice of Mitia's attempt to shoot himself.
	'BURNT BY THE SUN'	'The Weary Sun' (tango, original title 'Utomlennoe solntse'); diegetic: radio transmission	The music is integrated into the narrative through the announcement on the radio of a concert as requested by the peasant workers. It also creates a transition to the next episodes, which take the viewer into the peasant world (fields).

Mitia accepts a special assignment when he eventually answers the phone.	Mitia holds the telephone receiver while cold sweat stands on his forehead.		Mitia knows about the assignment he will be asked to take on; he is expected to give an answer only over the phone. The assignment is not a pleasant one, otherwise Mitia would not have attempted to shoot himself.
Nadia mutters the words of the song.	Blue sky. FILM TITLES Birch trees and a pavilion with a musical quartet in the snow. A man in a military overcoat and a woman (Kotov and Marusia) are dancing. Nadia is sitting on a bench, swinging her feet to the rhythm of the tango.	diegetic: 'The Weary Sun' played by the orchestra	Contrast of summer and winter, Moscow and countryside: a typical Russian landscape with birch trees. The title song echoes the theme of the absence of love. The tango was a popular genre in the 1930s, but would soon be considered decadent and replaced by Soviet marches.
	A boy is running through the yellow fields as the tanks are crushing the crop into the mud (camera pans from panorama shot to close-up).	diegetic: tank engines	The wheat (grain) is the pride of the peasants. This scene shows the countryside in a glorified perspective, since the 1930s were characterized by famines and crises in the management of collective farms.

	Action	Sound	Commentary
	In the bathhouse (*bania*) Nadia sits on Kotov's back and lashes him with birch twigs. She is tired and rests on his shoulders. Marusia washes clothes in a bowl as Kotov flirts with her. Nadia does the 'platypus': she pulls her upper lip up to her nose.	diegetic: lashing later some guitar tunes (non-diegetic)	The choice of the setting is typically Russian: the bathhouse. The theme of family happiness is conventional.
People are shouting that the tanks should leave the fields.	The tanks are approaching the fields with the crop about to be harvested. Children run up to the tanks. The Lieutenant watches a signalman through a field glass.	diegetic: noise of engines; the shouting of the peasants	The tanks represent a potential threat: could they be foreign, is this a war? The tanks are Russian. The view through the field glass suggests that the army is in control, while it takes no notice of the needs of the people.

2 Dialogue	Image	Sound/Music	Commentary
The truck driver asks the rider for the way to Zagorianka. The rider sends him back the other way; he is in a rush already at 7 a.m. The driver moans about his wife who washed his shirt without checking the content of his pockets; now the address has been washed out of the paper.	A man on horseback rides along a road by the river, and passes by the truck at the crossroads. After a short dialogue between the rider and the driver the truck turns round.	diegetic: tramping of horse; engine of truck	The rider diverts the truck and stops him from driving into the manoeuvre and causing more havoc in the fields.
	Mokhova, in her room in the dacha, takes pills; her cupboard is full of medicine jars and bottles. Drawings of hands decorate the walls.		The taking of pills refers to the suspicion of medication in the Stalin period when there were numerous incidents of poisoning. The drawings of hands allude to Mokhova's fear of men grabbing her breasts. She is a spinster. The dacha setting has a pre-Revolutionary and bourgeois character. The dacha is built of wood, not stone (like the Moscow house), but offers modern conveniences (a bathroom) alongside the traditional *bania* (steam-bath).
Mokhova tells the rider that Kotov is not to be disturbed.	The horseman rides through the village streets decorated with red flags, and up to the gate of Kotov's dacha where he leaves his horse. He runs to the house and knocks at the door, then at the window. Mokhova opens the window and speaks with him. Olga Nikolaevna wakes up and appears on the balcony.		

The villagers shout at the soldiers in the tanks that they are destroying the harvest.	The villagers assemble around the tanks, while an old woman hits one tank with a stick and throws her basket at the tank's driver.		The people defend themselves: the strength of the people against state power is underlined.
The rider asks Kotov to come and stop the tanks. Kotov is the only person who can help, since the village chairman is at a meeting about the dirigible. Kotov complains that he is being disturbed on his only day off.	The rider runs up to the bathhouse and opens the door. Kotov chases him away, but comes out of the bathhouse and gets dressed. Then Kotov runs down the slope, mounts a horse, and rides off.		Kotov is flattered: he is the only person who can help. The fuss he makes about his only day off is not serious. Kotov is ready to lend his forceful voice to express the otherwise unsanctioned will of the people.
	Marusia and Nadia leave the bathhouse to follow Kotov. Kotov on horseback, riding through the wood. He rides up to the tanks. The lieutenant looks through the field-glass to see the signals.	non-diegetic: triumphant trumpet music (composed by Artemiev) begins	Kotov as potential hero.
Kotov shouts at the soldiers in the tanks and asks why they are destroying what the people have sowed. The soldiers are only following orders from the commanding lieutenant.	The lieutenant sees Kotov through the field glass and walks up to him.		The soldiers only carry out orders, blindly and despite better knowledge from peasant experience.

The lieutenant tells Kotov to get out of the way, while Kotov gives him orders. The lieutenant continues to swear abusively at Kotov when the latter suggests that perhaps the lieutenant has not recognized him?	Kotov borrows a soldier's cap and poses in profile: the lieutenant recognizes Kotov and stands to obey orders.	Kotov is an important man: his portrait is what people recognize. Kotov shows fairness when he gives the lieutenant a chance to recognize him.
	Kotov finds out who the chief commander is: Misha Lapin. He asks for a connection to be made on the field phone.	
	The signal flags go down and aeroplanes fly over the fields. Kotov and the lieutenant run to the field radio. Marusia with Nadia, both in white, watch from far off in the fields. Kotov waves with child-like enthusiasm at the aeroplanes. An aerial view shows the mud and the people.	The beauty of aircraft: aerial control in the context of the conquest of the Soviet territory. The supremacy of aircraft to tanks: they do not destroy the harvest, and with their 'steel wings' ('Aviators' March') they represent technological progress.
Kotov speaks with the commander and mocks the grand scale of the manoeuvre. He tells Lapin to think of another solution for the exercise. Kotov asks the lieutenant for his name, but the latter is so confused that he says 'Misha, no, Kolia'. Kotov apologizes for having been so harsh.	The lieutenant smiles and grins under the impact of the encounter with Kotov.	The impact of the encounter with Kotov on the simple soldier makes him forget who he is. (Similar effect of encounters with Stalin.) Kotov apologizes – although as a commander he need not do so – to the lieutenant, and calls him Kolia. Kotov is a fair military man.

Artemiev's non-diegetic music ends

		lyrical tune (non-diegetic)	
Marusia tells Kotov that she has never heard him so angry. Nadia has not heard anything…	Nadia and Marusia smile proudly as the tanks move back. Kotov goes up to them and they walk back home together, as Kotov carries Nadia on his shoulders. The tanks withdraw. The kitchen at the dacha: Kotov washes his face while Marusia passes him the towel, laughing.		The image of Marusia and Nadia dressed in white offers parallels to the portrait of a madonna with her child in the fields.
Kotov reproaches Olga Nikolaevna for having told the rider where to find him. Kotov argues that he has interfered in what is not his business, and that Lapin could have refused his request, which was, after all, a personal favour. Vsevolod Konstantinovich misunderstands what Kotov says, taking literally the phrase 'vstavit' arbuz' ('to put a melon up', here meaning 'to refuse') and claiming this is not the time for melons. Olga Nikolaevna prefers a decent bathroom to the Russian steam-bath. She tells Vsevolod that he is complacent.	Olga Nikolaevna wears a white gown and goes back and forth, while Vsevolod's feet are in her way. Vsevolod is reading the newspaper. Mokhova is laying the table, singing.		The family have no interest in Kotov's status and rank. Kotov's use of language is different from that of Marusia's family.
			Kotov is a stranger in this house: his conduct differs (bathhouse and bathroom).

3 Dialogue	Image	Sound/Music	Commentary
Nadia is told off by Mokhova for putting her finger in the jam. She asks the old ladies what they are doing.	Nadia sings and dances in the corridor. She goes into the music room, says hello to the budgerigars. She looks out of the window and sees the old ladies walking to the river.	diegetic: Nadia sings 'Weary Sun'; the budgerigars are twittering	Nadia is cheeky with adults.
The old ladies comment that the medicines were brought by Boris before the Revolution. Mokhova is obsessed with medicines: when the doctor prescribed iron she dissolved some nails in water and drank the liquid. They are worried she might poison herself.	Elena and Lidia descend to the river and throw away some pills. They signal Nadia to be quiet.	twittering of birds	The transition from inside to outside is made through the birds chirping and Nadia's view through the window. Again, the theme of poisoning resounds.
The truck driver asks Liuba whether this is Zagorianka. Liuba is irritated, since she thinks this is KhLAM. Kirik confirms that the village is called KhLAM – meaning 'trash'.	The camera captures the feet of a woman: Liuba is walking along a village road. The truck stops, the driver talks to Liuba. Kirik rides past on his bike.		Both the driver and Liuba are looking for the way and are temporarily disoriented.

Inside the dacha the family gather at the dining table, which has rattan furniture; they are all dressed in white and light blue. Kotov finds a trumpet, which the pioneers have brought. [As the family sit at the table, Kotov sits in a rocking chair. Nadia blows into the trumpet. Kotov looks through the mail, reads a letter and gives one to Marusia. Elena shows a coat she is making.] Mokhova's medicine cupboard is empty (close-up).	Olga calls Elena. Kotov chases Nadia from his chair. Vsevolod talks about 'confession as a source of justice', and is told by Olga to stop commenting on political matters. [Vsevolod asks Olga to cut his hair. He mentions purges at the faculty. Nadia asks Vsevolod to play the trumpet. Kotov comments on Elena's coat.]		The trumpet as a Soviet military instrument is juxtaposed to the piano music and the literary quotes of the intelligentsia. The frame showing the empty cupboard explains why Mokhova is crying. [The threat of purges is looming. Kotov sits away from the table: he is an outsider in the family context.]
Mokhova lies on her bed, crying.	The old ladies are worried about Mokhova.	diegetic: crying	Mokhova is a cry-baby.
Kotov does the 'platypus' with Nadia. Kirik arrives on his bike, bringing biscuits. Marusia leaves the room with a letter in her hand. Kirik puts on a record and Nadia begins to dance.	Kirik congratulates everybody on the occasion of the holiday. Elena defends her son Kirik against Kotov's remark that he drinks.	diegetic: record with 'Weary Sun'	Kirik is a performer, clown, fool.

Kirik compares Vsevolod to the eternal student Petia Trofimov in *The Cherry Orchard*. Vsevolod is the eternal professor. Olga asks Kirik whether he has returned the money he borrowed from the saleswoman. She prompts Kirik in his reply to Kotov concerning alcohol. [Kirik comments on the coat. Kotov reminds Kirik to return the five roubles he borrowed from Marusia.]	Nadia dishevels Vsevolod's hair. Kirik sits with Olga and flirts: he holds some greens in his mouth like a flower, while Olga eats an apple. Nadia stands by the gramophone and does the 'platypus'. [Kirik is upset about Kotov's remark about the money and leaves the room.]	diegetic: song on record; Nadia accompanies the voice on the record.	Nadia is now in her own world, not that of the adults.
Liuba introduces herself as a colleague of Vsevolod's. If Kirik had known she was coming here, he would have taken her on the bike, but his is a girl's bike. Kotov invites everybody to go for a swim. Liuba meets Kotov for the first time in real life, having seen only his portraits: she is impressed	Construction site of the dirigible with workers. Red flags and a banner with the words 'Glory to the Builders of Stalin's Airships'. Liuba sits with Vsevolod at a small table. Vsevolod reads her essay. Kirik joins them. Kotov walks through the room and Kirik salutes when Kotov suggests that they go swimming. Kirik throws kisses at Liuba.	diegetic: hammering	Soviet reality outside: the concern with airships, reflecting the desire to construct a tool that allows domination and control, whilst it is fragile and more ephemeral than, say, an aeroplane. Kirik is a womanizer, who also borrows money from everybody. Kotov is again shown to be very much admired and known from his portraits.

4 Dialogue	Image	Sound/Music	Commentary
Nadia comforts Mokhova, promising that Kotov will bring her new medicine. Nadia hears the pioneers' marching and appeals to Mokhova to 'be a pioneer and stop crying'. Elena and Lidia do not know which holiday it is, but Nadia knows all the Soviet celebrations.	Mokhova fishes the tablets from the water with a net. Nadia stands by her and watches, then she runs to the gate. She pulls over a bench to stand on it so that she can see over the top of the fence. Elena and Lidia are in their room, measuring a coat. A sewing machine is standing by the window. They lie down for a rest.	diegetic: march music in the distance	Nadia wants to be a pioneer. She shows compassion for others. They make a coat themselves: this activity which is a-typical of the intelligentsia shows how far they have fallen on the social ladder; they cannot even afford to buy ready-made clothes.
	The pioneers follow a portrait of Stalin, which is carried along the street. Nadia is standing at the gate and salutes. Last in the parade is an old man (Mitia in disguise) with a trumpet, sporting a beard and sunglasses. He stops, sniffs around, then goes towards Nadia.	diegetic: 'Aviators' March' played by the brass band of marching pioneers	The lines 'We are born to make the fairy-tale come true' in the 'Aviators' March' foreshadows Mitia's role as a story-teller; it also echoes the 'steel wings' of the aeroplanes that dominate and explore the territory of the expanding Soviet state.

The old man knows Nadia's name and praises her as a future model pioneer girl. He introduces himself as a magician from the Maghreb, the country of summer Santas. Nadia asks whether this is a Soviet land and whether winter Santas live there too. She wonders whether he may also be a doctor who could help Mokhova.	Nadia looks at the old man through the fence.	diegetic: birds twittering	Nadia is a child: she is interested in fairy tales, and lets the magician into the house despite having been told not to open the gate. Again, she shows compassion for Mokhova in trying to find her a doctor. Soviet reality is integrated into fairy tales: Santas must necessarily live in the Soviet Union.
The old man reminds Olga that she once wiped Marusia's buttocks; he addresses the old ladies as grandmothers; he calls Vsevolod a polygamist and Kirik a lover of sweet wines and young women; he quotes Kotov's old telephone number at the OGPU.	Nadia leads the old man into the house, where he looks into every room. He grabs Mokhova's breasts; he goes up to everybody as they emerge from different rooms, but backs away from Marusia. He goes to the piano and everybody gathers around him in great bewilderment.	non-diegetic: piano tunes	Mitia's arrival is another intrusion after the earlier incident of the horseman finding Kotov in the bathhouse. A carnivalesque scene of arrival, which Mitia needs to return to his past. The phrase he addresses to Olga is a reminder of how Boris cared about his baby daughter. Marusia knew that Mitia was back in Russia from the letter, hence she knows immediately who the old man in disguise is.

The family welcome Mitia. Marusia introduces Mitia to Kotov, whom he has met before, and to Nadia.	Mitia is sitting at the piano, playing and singing. Marusia looks at the mirror in which she sees Mitia, who takes off the beard and the dark glasses. He wears a grey jacket. Everybody kisses and welcomes Mitia; Mitia and Marusia pile up their hands as a gesture of welcome. Vsevolod, followed by Mokhova, comes in. Mitia climbs onto a chair and finds a toffee on the cupboard, placing it on Mokhova's tray. The family leave the music room for the dining room.	diegetic: Puccini played on the piano	The handshake between Marusia and Mitia reflects what they have in common: a gesture, just like the 'platypus' gesture between Kotov and Nadia.
Mitia asks Mokhova whether she has been dusting the place properly: he hid a toffee away at the New Year Party in 1927/28. Mokhova takes this as an insult and leaves in tears.			Again, Mokhova is portrayed as a cry-baby. Mitia identifies the toffee as a mark he left in the house that was once his home.

Mitia asks for some water. Olga enquires from upstairs about Mitia: he is married with three children and works as a musician. Vsevolod wants to ask what Mitia has been doing all these years, but is told by Olga to be silent. Nadia asks Mitia whether he wants tea with jam or coffee with milk; Mitia would like coffee with jam. Mitia remembers a visit to the Bolshoi Theatre when Marusia was six, and how he had to take her to the toilet five minutes after the performance had started. Kirik asks Mitia for money.

Marusia and Mitia leave the room last. Mitia fetches a towel from a drawer in the corridor and goes to the bathroom to wash his face. He throws his grey jacket to the side. Marusia fetches a glass of water: she runs the samovar tap until the water flows over the edge of the glass, and then she drinks it herself, taking the empty glass with her. Her wrists are scarred.

Kirik hands the towel to Mitia in the bathroom. Olga comes and catches Kirik accepting Mitia's money, which she snatches away from him.

Mitia knows the house well: he feels at home.

Most of the dialogue is off camera, which remains almost fixed on the empty corridor and people walking up to the bathroom to ask something of Mitia.

Marusia has attempted suicide. She is tense because of Mitia's presence: Mitia was the reason for her suicide attempt.

Mitia wants things he cannot have: both coffee and jam. Mitia's memory of Marusia as a child serves to take the tension away from her.

Olga controls Kirik, who again tries to borrow money. Mitia helps generously.

5 Dialogue	Image	Sound/Music	Commentary
Mitia continues his recollection of the theatre visit. Nadia points out that Mitia is sitting in Kotov's chair, but Kotov tells her off for offending a guest. Mitia will not have coffee, since he has only just had breakfast. Vsevolod tries to say something and is stopped by Olga. SILENCE Kotov suggests that they go for a swim. Lidia says that Mitia has not changed at all, but his hair looks different. She asserts that nothing has changed, and they are too old to change anyway. Kotov is welcomed by the bathers at the beach.	The family resume their seats at the table and Mitia emerges from the bathroom to join them. Marusia sits aside, while Mitia sits in Kotov's rocking chair. Marusia nervously clinks her fingers on her glass and Olga draws her attention to this. Marusia puts the glass on the table, while Olga begins to tap nervously with her fingers at the side of the plate. Only Nadia is eating and drinking. Marusia rushes out of the room at the first opportunity.		Nadia is cheeky again, telling Mitia not to sit in Kotov's chair. Marusia is nervous and tense, as is Olga. Mitia remembers only a childhood adventure in which Marusia was mistaken for a boy.
	The camera offers a panorama shot of the wood and the river banks. The family, all dressed in white, walk down to the beach. The pioneers are also on their way to the beach.	diegetic: the amplifier at the beach with a radio announcement of a concert at 17.00 to commemorate the sixth anniversary of the Day of Dirigibles and Aeronautics	Soviet reality outside: agitation and propaganda, pioneers and holidays, practice of voluntary organizations (e.g. 'Osoaviakhim', the Society for the Support of Aviation and Chemical Construction).

Nadia refuses to play with the doll: she is a big girl. She tells Mitia that she wants to be a pioneer ('get up at the bugle's call, swim at the whistle's blast...'); Mitia adds to this list: 'march to the drum's beat, eat in time, and if you do all that well, you get buried to music, too.'	Mokhova gives Nadia a doll to play with. The pioneers prepare for a swim in the river. Mitia sits on the ground, Marusia lies in the sun. Kotov stands to one side. Mitia and Kotov take their shoes off simultaneously. Kotov's bare feet are next to a broken bottle.	diegetic: Soviet music	The danger of the broken bottle: Kotov is unharmed by it; Mitia worries about Nadia stepping onto the glass, but she too goes by unharmed without even noticing the potential threat.
Marusia tells Nadia not to bother Mitia with questions. Nadia goes towards Kotov, but Mitia calls her back, then letting her go all the same. Nadia complains to Kotov about having been told off, but he explains that Marusia and Mitia are old friends who want to be alone. He will take her in the boat. Marusia does not like this and turns away. Mitia can understand Marusia's admiration for Kotov, whose portraits are everywhere, but warns her that this image may collapse.	Mitia and Kotov make gestures to each other. Nadia leaves the doll with Mitia when she is sent away by Marusia and called by Kotov.	lyrical tune (non-diegetic)	Nadia's response is genuinely child-like: her curiosity, her upset at being told off.
	Mitia looks through the broken bottle and throws the glass away. Nadia and Kotov sit by the jetty. Then they take a boat.	diegetic: announcement about a lost white poodle	Kotov comforts Nadia: they have a good father–daughter relationship.
	Mitia and Marusia lie in the sun. The pioneers stand in formation.	diegetic: accordion music	

The scar on Mitia's shoulder indicates that he too has fought in the war. On Kotov's body we see only tattoos. Mitia and Marusia joke with each other.

[Mitia holds the doll on his palm. Olga sits in a deck chair. Mitia and Marusia lie on a blanket.]

[Mitia remembers how Marusia clasped his finger as a baby. Marusia discovers a scar on Mitya's shoulder, and Mitia claims 'a coffin-lid' dropped on him. Mitia mocks the volume of the radio.]

6 Dialogue	Image	Sound/Music	Commentary
Marusia does not want to know what happened to Mitia. She says she cut her wrists when he left, but did not know that it has to be done in water. The old women warn about the Civil Defence Unit approaching.	Mokhova is drawing her own hand. Mitia is chewing a straw and looking across Marusia's body. Marusia is reading a book. Mitia sees that Marusia has scars on her wrists. The old ladies are sitting on the grass under an umbrella. Mitia lies next to Marusia and smokes a cigarette (*papirosa*). The Civil Defence Unit approaches from the other side of the river. Nadia and Kotov on the boat.	diegetic: the pioneers recite songs to the accordion; sound of grass in the wind	There is no common ground between Marusia and Mitia other than the past.
Kotov looks at Nadia's rosy heels and says that the Soviet people are building roads and transport to make sure that heels like hers stay rosy. Nadia tells Kotov how much she loves him.		non-diegetic: musical theme 'Father and Daughter' by Artemiev	Kotov instils in Nadia an appreciation of Soviet values.

A fat woman bather asks Mitia for the time (1.30 p.m.).		
Marusia leaps up to go for a swim. Mitia pretends to be an invalid and is helped up by the fat lady. He runs in his clothes to the river and jumps in; then he dives for a long time and Marusia looks out for him, becoming worried. There are currents in the water. Marusia jumps in, and Mitia scares her by pulling her feet from below. They get out of the water on the other side of the river.	diegetic: Soviet jazz from the radio	Mitia plays games with Marusia, they behave like children. Mitia is a 'performer' in everything he does.

7 Dialogue	Image	Sound/Music	Commentary
Mitia remembers how he found Marusia by the river after she had discovered an affair between Kirik and her mother a month after her father had died. She had run away then. Mitia quotes a passage from *Hamlet* ('Ere yet the salt of most unrighteous tears / Had left the flushing in her galled eyes'). He remembers the night they spent together, and the trace of the elastic on her tummy. Now, at the dacha, everything had stayed the same, only without him: Mitia has been effaced from that life.	At first Mitia looks at Marusia, then he leans on a tree and Marusia looks in another direction. Mitia tries a forced smile when he gets no response from Marusia.		Marusia turns away when Mitia recalls the past: she is still too emotionally involved even to look at him. He does not take the opportunity to embrace her: he does not want to get involved again.
At the beach people are asked to put on the gas masks supplied by the Unit. The fat woman needs to catch a train. Marusia returns to the beach and reports that she is injured. Mitia follows her and claims to be dead (for the evacuation practice).	The gas attack evacuation practice is under way: men and dogs wear gas masks. The fat woman falls off a stretcher. Marusia lies on a stretcher and is carried away. Mitia steps onto the glass and, now really injured, is also carried off on a stretcher with a woman from the Unit whom he drags along. [The Unit manager now has the beach to himself.]	diegetic: sound of sirens; Soviet marches over the amplifier	The evacuation exercise is parodied: the dogs wear gas masks; Mitia makes a mocking comment about the music; and finally the officer uses the beach for himself, against the collective spirit.

Nadia moans about what would have happened to her had she left all the things at the beach. Kotov rushes Nadia home, and asks her to hang their things up to dry.		
Kotov and Nadia return to find everyone gone. They collect the things left there. Kotov rushes home through the woods and birch trees; he carries Nadia since she cannot walk fast enough. At the dacha Mitia's clothes are hanging on the line. Kotov rushes into the house.	diegetic: birds	Kotov suspects that Mitia and Marusia have rekindled their affair.
Kotov runs upstairs and listens at a door from which groaning noises can be heard. Kirik and Liuba are inside, pumping up a ball.	diegetic: heavy breathing and sounds similar to the squeaking of a bed	Kotov's suspicion of an affair is mocked: the sounds of the squeaking and breathing stem from the pumping up of the football.

8 Dialogue	Image	Sound/Music	Commentary
Olga remembers that Boris had asked his most talented student, Mitia, to become Marusia's music teacher. Often they would play the cancan instead of classical music and scales.	Old photographs decorate the room, but between these are newer pictures of Kotov. Nadia watches Marusia and Mitia, both wearing gas masks, play the piano. Mitia wears a red gown, Marusia a white dress. When they begin the cancan, Marusia takes off the gas mask and gets up to dance. Liuba runs down from upstairs to join in the dance. Gradually, everybody is dancing the cancan. Only Kotov stands on the threshold and watches.	diegetic: classical music on the piano, then cancan	Kotov has broken into Marusia's world: his photographs have merged with those of Marusia's family, whilst Kotov remains an outsider to their culture and family jargon.
Kotov cannot speak French and therefore, he claims, could not ask the others to lunch. Mokhova calls everybody in French.	Kotov sits down at the dining table and starts lunch. Mokhova stares at him.	diegetic: thunder claps	Kotov has no education and is a stranger in his own family. Threat of thunder.

Marusia gets Mitia's clothes.		Off screen, then, the scene that makes Marusia laugh: Mitia is sitting at the piano, wearing a gas mask; he takes off the gown and flings it over a chair; he is (almost) naked whilst wearing the mask, when Marusia brings in his clothes. Marusia's embarrassment shows that she still loves him.
The family all dance into the dining room. Mitia plays faster and faster. Marusia brings him his dry clothes, while Mitia flings his gown across the room. Marusia stands at the door and looks at him for a moment, then throws his clothes at him and runs off, laughing and embarrassed.	diegetic: cancan and classical music played on the piano non-diegetic: lyrical tune	
The truck driver is chased away. The address is illegible because his wife washed his shirt.		The theme of effacement links with the earlier reference from Mitia: he has been effaced from Marusia's life, just as the address has been effaced from the truck driver's note.
The truck stops at the airship construction site as the banner is being attached to the balloon.	diegetic: hammering	
Elena used to sing on stage in the old times. Vsevolod says that the taste of life has gone forever.	Elena sings an aria from *Madame Butterfly*	Mitia belongs with the family; Kotov looks out of place.
They all sit round the table.		

9 Dialogue

[Kotov challenges Vsevolod's comments about the happy past and asks why the intelligentsia did not defend their values, but ran away from the illiterate Bolsheviks. Kotov has never studied, just as Kirik never served in the army.]

Mitia asks Nadia for her name in French: Nadine. Nadia quibbles, claiming it is Nadja. Mitia tells 'Nadja' a fairy tale about Yatim, a good singer and musician, and the magician Sirob, who took him on like a son. Sirob had a daughter, Yasum. They were a happy household ('like ours, no, like yours') until the war (not against anyone in particular), when Yatim had to leave for the front. He was injured, then went abroad, but never forgot the house or even the budgerigars ('not the ones in the other room'). Yatim

Image

[Kotov gets up as he argues with Vsevolod. Mitia leaves the room and goes to the piano, where he sits and smokes. The camera pans over family photos and pictures of Kotov.]

Mitia is in the adjacent room and looks into the dining room through a window. Mitia lifts Nadia into the music room through the window. Both are seen through the window. Mitia on the right, Nadia on the left. Mitia places three dolls in the centre section of the tripartite window which has a curtain: a small, naked doll for Yatim, a taller one in a dress for Yasum. When he talks about leaving for the war, Mitia changes chairs so that his face is covered by the net curtain.

Sound/Music

non-diegetic: piano tunes

Commentary

During and after the Revolution the intelligentsia did not defend their ideas and values. Now they have only memories and snapshots of the past.

Mitia uses the standard phrases for a fairy tale, and Nadia responds entirely within the genre: she assumes there will be a happy ending, and suspects the important man is a bogeyman or an ogre, the standard characters of a fairy tale.

Yet she also shows signs of her Soviet upbringing: the war must have been against the 'nobbles' (Nadia's word for the bourgeoisie).

Again, Nadia is torn between her child-like belief in the narrative, and the attempt to turn herself into a Soviet girl, played the piano in restaurants and danced in cabarets, and when he returned ten years later his parents had died. He went to his teacher's house, (1) and Yasum opened the door. (2) Nadia claims to know the end of the story: Yatim and Yasum will marry. Mitia disappoints Nadia's expectation: an important man (a bogeyman or an ogre) arrived (3) and sent Yatim away, although Yatim just wanted to be happy; but he was not allowed such 'bourgeois' thoughts. (4) Yatim had to write a note, otherwise he would have been beheaded.

Mitia leaves the room when he talks about having left the country, and returns after having drunk Kirik's vodka and lit a cigarette.
The moment of Yasum opening the door is enacted with the dolls. Marusia's hand holding a cup is shaking.

The FIREBALL passes (1) OVER THE RIVER, (2) THROUGH BIRCH TREES, (3) INTO THE HOUSE and (4) INTO THE ROOM, passing the door frame on which the height of Mitia and Marusia at different ages is marked.

a future pioneer, as earlier with the Santas (when she queried whether the disguised Mitia was a Soviet Santa). The inversion of names in Russian needs to be seen in connection with the inversion theme linked with the 'Aviators' March' (We are born to turn a fairy tale into reality).

10 Dialogue	Image	Sound/Music	Commentary
Yatim left the house without telling anyone, because he wanted to protect the family, and because he wanted to live. (5) Yasum cried, and later married the important man whose name he cannot remember. (6)	When Mitia says that Yasum cried, he takes the guitar and plays 'Weary Sun'. (5) PICTURE GLASS BURSTS and then the fireball (6) LEAVES THE HOUSE and goes INTO THE WOODS.	diegetic: Nadia sings and Mitia plays 'Weary Sun'	The fireball destroys one single tree at the moment when Mitia speaks of having lost his love, his former life, the meaning of his existence. The destruction is accidental: one tree in the woods. A parallel is created between the life of a tree and that of a human being (the bond between man and nature). Kotov manifests his physical power over Marusia, especially in a situation where she is upset, to the point of being suicidal.
	Marusia runs upstairs, and Kotov follows her. A silent argument takes place between them. Marusia prepares to jump out of the window when Kotov takes his clothes off and draws Marusia toward him; Marusia cries on Kotov's shoulder. The fireball HITS and BURNS ONE TREE.	non-diegetic tune	

Nadia tells Mitia that they will play football later: croquet and tennis are bourgeois games, but football is a collective game. Kotov has promised to take Nadia on the following day to the zoo, where she has been only in winter when most of the animals are asleep. Mitia suspects that Nadia smells of wine, but it turns out that this is Kirik. Nadia criticizes Kirik, who sends her away to play.

Mitia looks at the pictures of the past and of Kotov. Nadia is sitting at the table, drawing. The marks on the door frame are shown: Mitia 1916, Marusia 14 years. Kirik is in the kitchen and drinks wine. Mitia measures himself now and writes 'Yatim, 36 years'. Nadia's mark is there, too, and he writes 'Yadan' next to her name.

Mitia admits to Kirik that he is not married, but has made up his biography; in reality, he serves in the NKVD, but Kirik believes that he is joking again. Kirik manages film projection in a sanatorium; he asks why Mitia did not come earlier, and explains what happened to Marusia after he had left. Kirik is turning bald, and he relates his loss of hair to smoking; Kirik therefore does not smoke, unlike Mitia, who has a head of full hair. Kirik suggests that Mitia should resume his affair with Marusia.

Kirik and Mitia are in the sitting room. Mitia hits Kirik when he suggests he could rekindle his affair with Marusia, and pulls Kirik's hairnet over his face.

Mitia is sincere with Kirik: they are both performers and speak the same language.

11 Dialogue	Image	Sound/Music	Commentary
	Marusia lies on top of Kotov as they are making love in the attic.		
	A black car appears behind the trees.		
	Mitia and Nadia are sitting at the piano, playing a simple tune together.	diegetic: piano music	Mitia gets on well with Nadia, as he must have done with Marusia when she was little. Kotov argues that there is always a choice, even if in Mitia's case the price was life. He places duty above all.
Kotov admits that he sent Mitia away. For Kotov there is always a choice: Mitia could have refused. Kotov suggests that they move to a state dacha to avoid intrusions from the outside world and from the past. Kotov would leave his family if it was necessary: he is a military man who acts for love of his country and through duty, not fear.	Marusia's head rests on Kotov's shoulder as they are lying in the hay.		
Mitia asks whether Nadia can tap-dance.	Mitia and Nadia are still at the piano. Mitia gets up and carries Nadia to the staircase.		Playing the piano and tap-dance are both 'bourgeois' pastimes. Mitia subverts Nadia.
Kotov asks Marusia to make a clicking sound with her tongue.	Kotov and Marusia are lying in the hay.		A common gesture also characterizes the relationship between Marusia and Kotov: Marusia makes a clicking sound with her tongue.

Mitia tells Marusia that he will leave soon, and asks to speak to Kotov. Mitia tells Nadia a secret: he will be picked up by a car in the evening.	Mitia is teaching Nadia tap-dance when Marusia comes down the stairs. He also teaches Nadia how to hold the note u-u-u-u. A conversation between Kotov and Mitia is observed by Marusia from behind the glass door, without being heard.	diegetic: sound of tapping	The spectator can only guess what Mitia tells Kotov: the conversation takes place behind the shut glass door, inaudible to the viewer and to Marusia.
Kotov asks Mitia not to say a word to anyone. He suggests that they play football since there are two hours left.	Kotov, Mitia and Nadia each perform a tap-dance.	diegetic: sound of tap-dance	Kotov's 'choice': he does not tell anyone that he will leave, just as Mitia had not done ten years ago.

12 Dialogue	Image	Sound/Music	Commentary
A peasant enumerates the villages he knows in the area, and swears at the truck driver.	The truck is now in a field by a haystack, while a peasant chases the driver away, throwing sticks at him. The football match is played in the woods; the ball is kicked into the trees.	non-diegetic: jazz music of the 1930s	The theme of disorientation is continued.

Mitia reminds Kotov of his impending arrest. Kotov asks Mitia why he did not mention in his story that in 1923 he himself became a secret agent of the OGPU, and denounced eight White officers. Mitia claims that he was forced to do so, but Kotov alleges that he was bought. Kotov has taken everything away from Mitia, and Kotov interprets Mitia's action as personal revenge. He is convinced that nobody will touch the legendary commander Kotov. Yet Mitia is convinced that Kotov will soon confess to having been a German spy since 1920 and a Japanese agent since 1923. If not, he will be reminded of his wife and child.
[The search of Kotov's property is scheduled for the next day. Kotov makes sure that Mitia's cheek is not hurting.]

Mitia follows Kotov, who goes looking for the ball. Kotov hits Mitia. Mitia resurfaces with the ball when Nadia (in a shirt with 'K' on it) comes looking for them. He holds his cheek. [Kotov and Mitia walk back together.]

Nadia's shirt has a 'K' (for Kotov) printed on it; this is a parallel to the 'D' on the shirts of the Dinamo football club (organized by Dzerzhinsky, founder of the secret service). Mitia refers to the interrogation practices of the NKVD: they will make Kotov confess whatever they want. Kotov is again fair when he shows concern for Mitia's cheek.

13 Dialogue	Image	Sound/Music	Commentary
The pioneers congratulate Kotov on the Holiday.	The pioneers stand in formation. Kotov salutes them, and so does Nadia. Kotov corrects her gesture. Mitia watches the scene from inside the house.	non-diegetic: piano tunes	Kotov teaches Nadia how to salute properly. The pioneers' discipline, their red ties and portraits of Stalin are the pride of the commander.
The driver asks Nadia whether this is number 9. Nadia was expecting the car. Nadia tells Mitia that the car has arrived. She asks him whether she can sit at the wheel when he leaves, and he agrees. Marusia asks Mitia why he told the fairy tale: Mitia recalls Boris's death and his last words about 'trains with geese'. Many things remain unsaid between Marusia and Mitia.	The black car arrives at the gate. Nadia watches from the gate and runs inside the house. Nadia comes running into the house. Mitia and Marusia remain alone in the room when Nadia goes off to find Kotov. A photo of Boris on the wall is caught by the camera. [Kotov is in his study, drinking brandy and looking at the photographs of himself and Stalin. He puts on a shirt.]	diegetic: crickets non-diegetic: piano tunes (Artemiev)	Nadia's joy at seeing the car is opposed to its mission: to arrest her father. 'Trains with geese' were the last words of Boris: all that remained of a rich and wonderful life is the absurd vision of birds on trains. The image may be read as one of 'poshlost'' (banality): people are carrying with them animals that can be eaten (the mundane concerns with food rather than ideals), whilst it is also a citation of the last words of Anton Chekhov's father before his death.

The three men in the car wonder whether this is Kotov's daughter. Nadia talks to them as they eat and drink. She informs them that she will come for a ride, and offers to bring them some cake, which they refuse. Nadia is called back to the house, and asks them not to say she has left the garden. Lidia tells Nadia that her father has called her. Elena is again late for tea. Nadia behaves like a boy.	The black car is parked in front of the gate. Nadia stands by the gate, then leaves the garden to go to the car (she knows she is not supposed to). She stands in front of the headlight to check how she looks. When called, Nadia runs back to the house and climbs through the window. Nadia jumps through the window and scares Lidia.	Nadia is both cheeky and charming in her attempt to approach the car and to confirm that she will really be allowed to sit at the wheel. The men refuse the cake she offers for fear of poisoning. Nadia behaves like a boy; Marusia was also mistaken for a boy in the episode related by Mitia. Parallels, drawn between mother and daughter, reflect also on Mitia's perception of Nadia as the spitting image of the young Marusia.
Nadia tells her father off for drinking without eating. Kotov tells her that he will leave with Mitia, since he has an engagement in Moscow early the next morning. Nadia tells him to hurry since she wants to sit at the wheel. She has worked out that she would be Yadan in the story.	Nadia sees her father in the mirror first, then smells her father's cup. Nadia helps Kotov put on his uniform. Kotov does the 'platypus' with Nadia.	Nadia transposes herself into the fairy-tale plot, but does not decipher the names of the other protagonists. She is excited about driving in the car to such an extent that she is not sad about her father leaving.

14 Dialogue	Image	Sound/Music	Commentary
Kotov will not be able to take Nadia to the zoo the next day. Nadia initiates a competition with Kotov, as to who can hold the u-note longest. She is little, so she allows herself to take a deep breath more often. [Vsevolod asks the men in the car who has sent this limousine. The men say they are from the regional philharmonic orchestra. Vsevolod sings some arias. Kotov tells Marusia that he will leave, and she queries why he is dressed in full uniform. Olga needs some cosmetics from Moscow.] Kirik speaks to the budgerigars who say 'the commander is a moron'. The old ladies invite the men in the car to have tea with them, but they refuse. Mitia orders Kotov to sit at the back so he can see better how Nadia steers.	Nadia and Kotov hold the u-note. Kotov stares at a picture of Stalin and himself. [Vsevolod stands by the car while the men inside the car are sweating. Inside the dacha Kotov gets ready to leave. Everybody leaves the house. The record on the gramophone has finished.] Kirik is standing by the birds' cage. Everybody goes to the gate. Nadia sits at the wheel. Then she gets out of the car and Kotov chases her around the car. Kotov carries both Marusia and Nadia along the street. Nadia returns to the car.	diegetic: u-note [diegetic: scratching needle on gramophone] non-diegetic: lyrical tune 'Father and Daughter' (Artemiev)	Kotov realizes that there is a potential danger: the pioneers may have praised him; he may have been close to Stalin, but maybe things have changed. He drinks. Everyday routine when Kotov leaves for Moscow. Mitia takes great care to make sure he does his job properly: Kotov must not sit at the front. Mitia keeps up appearances to a certain extent, but he controls each movement from now on.

	Sound	Commentary
[Mitia finds the *dachniki* have not sung together all day.] [Mitia and Marusia repeat their farewell (pile up their hands) and he kisses everybody good-bye as the women continue singing.] The car drives off, with Nadia at the wheel.	['Evening Bells']	Gestures form the common language between Marusia and Mitia. The folk tune emphasizes the sadness of departure, and connects with the non-Soviet legacy.
Mitia tells Alexei (the driver) to stop the car. Nadia jokes with the officers: have you been to the zoo? then why did you run away? did they not feed you well? Nadia is at the wheel, then the car stops in the fields. Nadia gets out and runs back through the fields.	non-diegetic: lyrical tune 'Father and Daughter' (Artemiev) diegetic: Nadia hums 'Weary Sun'	Nadia is again a cheeky girl when she mocks the officers.

15 Dialogue

Kotov proposes that they drink to the holiday and assures them that he has no intention of poisoning himself. He is asked to surrender his gun. [Kotov suggests that they sing a folk song and sings some tunes.] Kotov enquires where they are going, and invites Mitia to a restaurant. He laughs and claims he will call Stalin on the direct line and have their department investigated as soon as they get to Moscow. Mitia recalls the phrase 'trains with geese' and Kotov responds with the recipe: goose with apples. Kotov is reminded not to do anything stupid, but he confesses that he did something stupid years ago.

Image

The car drives on through the yellow fields. Kotov is seated in the middle on the back seat, between Mitia and an officer. He surrenders his pistol and drinks brandy. The truck blocks the road.

Sound/Music

Commentary

Kotov pretends to be in control. His drinking suggests, though, that he is not entirely sure.
He has now lost direction (he asks where they are going), just like the truck driver.

The truck driver has no petrol left and cannot find the village. Kotov says that maybe the place is 'Nagorie'. The driver recognizes Kotov.	The truck blocks the road and the car has stopped. Mitia and Alexei get out and the truck driver approaches the car, where he sees Kotov. Kotov wants to explain the way and get out of the car, but an officer holds him back. Kotov hits one of the officers and is then badly beaten up by all three officers. Mitia takes his coat and puts it on. The driver runs into the field but is called back.		Kotov suggests a name which implies a view, a perspective: 'On the Hill' (Na-gorie), not 'Behind the Hill' (Za-gor-ianka). Kotov begins the fight by hitting the officer: he does not take the situation seriously enough.
Mitia calls the driver back when he runs away and makes him stand by the truck with his hands up.			
The driver assures Mitia that he has all the relevant documents.	Mitia takes out a silver cigarette case. He is about to light a cigarette when the dirigible with Stalin's portrait rises. He is holding a match between his fingers, the cigarette between his lips, and salutes with an artificial and forced smile.	non-diegetic: 'Portrait of Stalin' (Artemiev)	Mitia has done his job. He does not believe in effigies, but his salute is a cynical homage.

The truck driver asks whether it is really Kotov in the car. Mitia claims that the man merely looks like Kotov.

Mitia returns to the car. He stops half-way to check the driver's papers. The men run up to the truck and the driver is shot. Mitia returns to the car, followed by the men. The bruised Kotov is handcuffed on the back seat. The car drives off. The mirror of a piece of furniture on the truck reflects the banner with Stalin, while the driver's dead body is hidden on the truck under a piece of tarpaulin.

The mirror on the truck deflects from reality: underneath lies the dead body.

16 Dialogue	Image	Sound/Music	Commentary
The officers praise Mitia for acting so swiftly and for figuring out that the truck was a ploy.	The car drives along the road towards the dirigible, then the balloon with the banner is visible through the side window of the car. Mitia looks at Kotov, who sobs. The portrait of Stalin covers part of the aerial view onto the fields, woods and the car.	Mitia whistles 'Weary Sun', some cello tunes (Artemiev)	The banner with Stalin's portrait covers almost the entire landscape and obscures the view.
	Mitia's flat, where Mitia lies in the bathtub. The FIREBALL enters through the window and glides over the piano. Mitia lies in the bathtub, the shaving knife lies on the edge. The water is stained red. The Kremlin towers are visible through the open window. The FIREBALL stands in the window, then leaves.	Mitia whistles 'Weary Sun'; Radio Moscow announces the time: 7 a.m.

the phone rings | 'Weary Sun' forms the transition between the last scene in the countryside and this scene in Moscow.
The phone ringing suggests that there may be more assignments waiting for Mitia: the NKVD will never let him off the hook.
The fireball indicates Mitia's physical destruction. |
| | Nadia runs home through the fields. | Nadia sings 'Weary Sun' | |

The characters

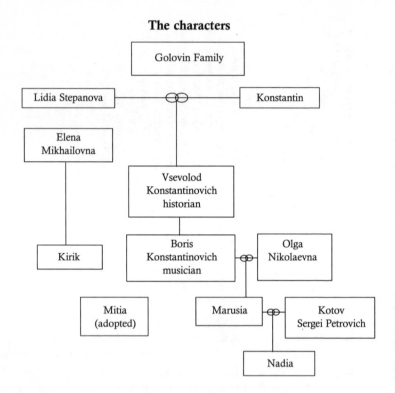

3. The Film and its Themes

Historical Background: Fact *v.* Fiction

Burnt by the Sun contrasts the pre-Revolutionary lifestyle of the intelligentsia (Marusia's father was a musician, her uncle is a professor of Roman Law in the Faculty of History) with that of the Soviet reality of Revolutionary leaders (Kotov). In their recollections the characters refer back to Russian history both before and after the Revolution.

The characters in Mikhalkov's film make a number of references to their past in relation to Soviet history; some are, indeed, victims of the turmoil after the Revolution or of the totalitarian system into which the Soviet state had turned under Stalin. This section aims to explain the historical context of the time in which the film is set.

Immediately after the October Revolution on 25 October (7 November, New Style) 1917 the Red Army met with resistance from those who had not supported the Bolshevik cause in the first place: former soldiers of the Imperial Army, together with other oppositional groups, made up the so-called 'White Army'. The Red Army had initially prevailed, but the White Army, supported by the Western Allies, continued to oppose the Bolsheviks. In 1918 the Whites advanced simultaneously on three fronts: from Siberia under Admiral Kolchak, under General Denikin from the South, and under Yudenich from the North; the Red Army, organized by the Commissar for War Lev Trotsky, defeated the Whites by late 1919, forcing the southern troops into retreat and finally evacuation (assisted by the Allied forces) to Constantinople around November 1920. The Reds controlled the central cities, Moscow and Petrograd; from the centre they conquered the periphery on which the Whites had concentrated their forces. This control of the centre by the Reds and the peripheral movements of the Whites is echoed and inverted in *Burnt by the Sun*: Mitia, the former White officer, now lives in Moscow, the centre of the Reds; Kotov, the Red Commander, lives (temporarily) in the countryside, in the domain of the 'Whites'. This shift of the Bolshevik Commander to the periphery, and the White officer rendering service to the Reds in the centre shows, on the one hand, the illusory nature of control; on the other hand, it anticipates who will be the winner and who the loser in the game of power that lies at the core of this film.

During those years of Civil War about two million people, mainly from the aristocracy, the bourgeoisie or the intelligentsia, fled from Russia whilst those who stayed in the country often fought in the ranks of the Whites. After the defeat of the Whites they had to emigrate as well, but many wanted to return to Russia. In order to efface their past with the White Army and to demonstrate their allegiance to the new communist regime they were forced to cooperate with the secret service before being allowed to return to Russia. An example that is now well-known to the intelligent Russian viewer and that offers many parallels to the biography of Mitia in the film is the case of Sergei Efron, the husband of the poet Marina Tsvetaeva. He had fought on the side of the Whites before emigrating to Germany in 1921. He later developed Soviet sympathies; as a token of his support for the new regime, he became a spy for the Soviet secret service. In 1937 he returned to the USSR, after he had been implicated in the murder of the former Soviet agent Ignat Reiss in Paris. Upon his return to the USSR he was arrested and shot.

The secret service had been established by Felix Dzerzhinsky in 1918 as the Cheka, the Extraordinary Commission for the Fight against Counterrevolution and Sabotage. It was reorganized in 1922 as the GPU (OGPU), the State Political Directorate, until July 1934, when it became the NKVD (People's Commissariat for Internal Affairs) headed by Genrikh Yagoda until 1936, then from 1936 to 1938 by Nikolai Yezhov, and later by Lavrenti Beria. In 1954 it was reorganized as the KGB (Committee for State Security), which was disbanded when the USSR collapsed in 1991.

The Civil War, together with the nationalization of the land and the practical suppression of private trade, had led to a destabilization of the economy. Lenin sought to remedy this situation with the New

Economic Policy (NEP), introduced in 1921 and lasting until the First Five-Year Plan of 1928. NEP allowed limited private trade and the management of privately owned land. After Lenin's death in 1924 NEP began to show its first results: trade, industry and agricultural produce were increasing. Stalin, who was in charge of Party membership, opposed NEP and advocated instead a socialist, collective management in all areas of the economy. On the political left Trotsky, supported by Grigori Zinoviev and Lev Kamenev, also opposed NEP, but they remained critical of Stalin's undemocratic management of the Party; on the right, Nikolai Bukharin pleaded for a compromise solution between communism and capitalism and a continuation of NEP. Amidst this pluralism of opinions concerning the management of the country Stalin secured at the Party Congress in 1927 a condemnation of any deviation from the Party line (as represented by Stalin himself). The Bolshevik leaders Zinoviev and Kamenev sided with Stalin, whilst Trotsky was expelled from the Party and deported in January 1929. He was assassinated in Mexico in 1940.

In the late 1920s signs of more rigid control also became apparent in the arts. Artistic movements were unified, and by 1934 the Writers' Union would proclaim socialist realism as the only mode of expression intelligible to the masses. Writers diverging from socialist realism, such as Anna Akhmatova and Boris Pasternak, found publication increasingly difficult. In other arts, too, only one line, one union, was tolerated: abstract art (Malevich) was condemned in favour of realism; experimentation with film form and montage (Eisenstein) was repressed whilst musical comedies for the masses were promoted; psychological realism on stage was canonized at the expense of Meyerhold's expressive interpretations of the classics; satirists (Erdman) were banned; and unconventional compositions in music (Shostakovich) were discredited. It is in August 1928 that Pasternak's Doctor Zhivago dies from 'lack of air' in an overcrowded trolleybus. This stifling process, which culminated in the 1930s, had begun in the late 1920s, just as Mitia returns from his exile in Paris to a country he does not recognize; the only thing he finds unchanged is Marusia's family home. Then he is forced by Kotov to leave again to carry out tasks for the secret service in Paris.

Throughout the 1930s purges were carried out in various spheres of life. In the early 1930s Stalin's programme of collectivization, designed to transform privately managed farms into state enterprises, cost a great many well-to-do farmers (*kulaks*) their lives. The purges of the Party apparatus were carried out in two stages: between 1928 and 1930, and again between 1933 and 1935 the lower ranks of the party were checked and double-checked, until new membership cards were issued in 1936. At the top level of the Party the process of 'clearing away' the old Bolsheviks who were potential rivals to Stalin was somewhat more complex. By 1934 dissatisfaction had grown among the delegates at the Party Congress and they supported Sergei Kirov, the head of the Leningrad Party Section, for the post of general secretary. When Kirov refused, the congress abolished the title 'general secretary', thus reducing Stalin's title to a post of one among equals. Indeed, in the ballot for Central Committee offices, 300 delegates voted against Stalin, whilst there were only three votes opposing Kirov's election to the Central Committee. The ballot papers were destroyed and the result of the vote hushed up. But Stalin's position had become insecure among his own comrades.

On 1 December 1934 Kirov was murdered; this act, it has been argued persuasively by both Russian and Western scholars, was a plot by Stalin and the NKVD devised to get rid of a potential rival because of Stalin's desire to establish absolute power for himself. The murder served as a pretext for empowering the NKVD with the right to trial and execution, thus paving the way for the Great Terror. Kirov's murder confirmed the absolute power of the new regime, while it also revealed that the ideals and beliefs of the new system were finally shattered: a series of arrests and trials followed at the top level of the Party. Zinoviev and Kamenev were arrested in December 1934, and put on trial for the first time in January 1935; however, they recanted and were not sentenced. There were further arrests of other high-ranking members of the Party. Forced denunciations and confessions, and expulsions from the Party soon became the order of the day. The lawyer Andrei Vyshinsky was appointed Chief Prosecutor in 1935 to preside over the show trials (in the 1950s he would rise to the post of Soviet representative at the United Nations). A circular accusing the Trotskyite-Zinovievite counter-Revolutionary centres of terrorist activities led to the first of the Moscow show trials in August 1936 when Zinoviev and Kamenev were implicated in the murder of Kirov; they were sentenced and executed on 24 August 1936; the chief prosecutor in their trial was Vyshinsky. On the basis of

Zinoviev's and Kamenev's confessions other high-ranking Party officials and ideologues were arrested. In January 1937 the case against Radek and Piatakov was brought to trial, and finally in March 1938 Bukharin and Yagoda (the former NKVD head) were tried. By the end of the purges Stalin had achieved an almost complete change of membership of the Central Committee between the Party Congresses of 1934 and 1939.

At approximately the same time, in July 1936, a military rebellion took place in Spain, overthrowing democracy and eventually making the leader of the Nationalist forces, General Franco, head of state. Franco's military dictatorship would last well beyond Stalin's leadership. Totalitarian regimes were now established across Europe, a point that adds a broader dimension to the events portrayed in the film.

Burnt by the Sun is set in June 1936, thus historically before the show trials. The radio transmission at the beginning of the film reports one of the show trials, with the concluding speech by Vyshinsky; the trial of Kamenev and Zinoviev did not take place until August 1936, whilst only the trial of Bukharin in 1938 was broadcast. According to the titles at the end of the film, Kotov is shot on 12 August 1936, thus even before the first show trial started. The film anticipates the Great Terror that would soon become manifest: while it is still possible for a high-ranking officer like Kotov to believe in the justice of the system, the threat is tangible, audible, and visible by the end of the film.

Finally, the question of historical accuracy arises: Mikhalkov chooses a specific Sunday in June 1936, although the yellow fields look much more as fields would in July. The Sunday is supposed to coincide with the day when Franco took power in Spain, 18 July (a Saturday, not a Sunday). The Day of Dirigibles and Aeronautics, too, is an invented holiday, although the evacuation practice echoes the widespread activities of such voluntary organizations as OSOAVIAKhIM (The Society for the Support of Aviation and Chemical Construction) in the 1930s. The film's preoccupation with the theme of aviation (military planes flying over the fields, the airship with Stalin's portrait, and the reference to the 'steel wings' in the 'Aviators' March') underscores a general significance of aviation in the 1930s: the view from above allowed for a better control of the territories. The red stars of the Kremlin, prominently framed in the film's opening and closing scene, were not put up until 1937 to mark the 20th anniversary of the October Revolution.[1]

The radio speech provides no historical reference point either, since the show trials began only in August and were in any case not recorded for broadcasting until 1938.[2] Mikhalkov creates an accurate time-frame that does not, however, hold up to detailed comparison against historical events. His deliberately fictional framework is coherent only within the film's narrative, while it is not designed to stand up to close historical scrutiny. Mikhalkov reminds the spectator in this way that the film is fiction, not fact, and that he is an artist, not a historian.

The emphasis is rather on capturing the last moments before the show trials made such a firm belief as Kotov's in Revolutionary ideals impossible, and to convey the atmosphere of a pre-Revolutionary lifestyle that really did survive into the 1930s in exceptional circumstances.[3]

Burnt by the Sun: Fact *v.* Fiction

Historical Fact	Year	Film Fiction
	1900	Mitia born
	1901	Philippe becomes Mitia's tutor
failed 'Revolution' which leads to the establishment of a parliament (Duma)	1905	
	1910	Marusia born
	1916	Marusia with Mitia at the Bolshoi Theatre
Bolshevik Revolution	1917	
Civil War	1918	Mitia fights in the White Army
Whites oppose Red Army and	–	
Bolshevik Government	1920	
Stalin: General Secretary for Party membership	1922	
OGPU recruits émigrés in return for allowing them to return to the Soviet Union	1923	Mitia recruited by OGPU; betrays White officers; exile to France
Lenin dies	1924	
	1926	Mitia returns to Russia (1926/27)
Deviation from Party line condemned	1927	Mitia leaves Russia for a second time
Trotsky expelled from Party and deported	1929	
	1930	Nadia born

Historical Fact	Year	Film Fiction
NKVD replaces OGPU	1934	
Writers' Congress: Socialist Realism (August)		
Murder of Kirov (December)		
Zinoviev and Kamenev arrested and imprisoned (January)	1935	
Death of Maxim Gorky (18 June)	1936	Mitia, now officer for the NKVD, returns to Moscow (January)
Soviet Constitution proposed (June)		Arrest of Kotov (June)
Yezhov's circular 'On terrorist activities of the Trotskyite-Zinovievite bloc' (29 July)		Arrest of Marusia and Nadia (June) Execution of Kotov (12 August)
Franco's military revolt (18 July)		
Margaret Mitchell's *Gone with the Wind* published (summer)		
Berlin Olympics (August)		
First show trial: Zinoviev and Kamenev executed (24 August)		
NKVD chief Yagoda replaced by Yezhov	1936	
Second show trial against Radek, Piatakov et al. (January)	1937	
Third show trial against Bukharin, Yagoda et al. (March)	1938	

Binary Oppositions

The title and names: double meanings

The working title for the film was *The Absolute Effect of the Fireball* [Bezuslovnyi effekt sharovoi molnii]. According to Mikhalkov the title was changed to *The Weary Sun of 1936* in the course of filming, since he did not like the consonant clusters in the first title. The final version of the title was inspired by an accidental mispronunciation by a caller enquiring when the film would be ready, and was immediately adopted.[4]

The film's title draws on the 1930s tango 'Utomlennoe solntse' (The Weary Sun), changing the grammatical correlation to *Utomlennye solntsem* – 'those who are made weary by the sun', those who are burnt by the sun of the Revolution. This is partly because of the rights held by the composer Jerzy Peterburgski, partly in order to create an assonance between 'Burnt by the Sun' and 'Gone with the Wind' (in Russian 'Unesennye vetrom' – 'those carried away by the wind').

There are only a few real events, figures and places that occur in the film, but a number of associative names, such as the placename 'Zagorianka' (the village which the driver is seeking), derived from the verb *zagoret* – to get sunburnt: if he comes too close to this place, he will get burnt: indeed, when he is about to be told how to get there, he is shot.

Kotov has no direct model in history, but the name is disyllabic, like that of Kirov, a figure whose popularity reveals certain parallels to Kotov; furthermore, both bear the Christian name Sergei. The name of Marusia's family, the Golovins, echoes not only that of the theatre director Meyerhold's famous set designer Alexander Golovin; it is derived from the Russian word *golova*, meaning head, which alludes to the intellectual background of Marusia's family.

Time and space

The film begins and ends with a view of the red stars on the Moscow Kremlin spires. The action of *Burnt by the Sun* departs from and returns to Moscow: NKVD officer Mitia arrives at his Moscow flat and accepts a special assignment. He travels to the country dacha to arrest Kotov, and brings him back to Moscow. Mitia's Moscow flat is located in the grey building that was the apartment house of the government, the 'House on the Embankment' featured in Trifonov's eponymous novella,[5] with a close view of the centre of political power (of the Reds), while the 'Whites' – the intellectual Golovin family – live on the periphery, on the outskirts, at least for the summer.

Burnt by the Sun operates within a closed circular structure in terms of time: the story begins at 6 a.m. and ends at 7 a.m. the following morning. If we remove the intersection of time and place, only one hour has elapsed between Mitia's attempt to shoot himself and his suicide in the bath. It could almost be that none of the events between the two suicide attempts had ever happened. The day portrayed in the film is a long and happy day for a little girl whose ideals remain unshattered throughout. In this, Nadia is not unlike the girl Svetlana from Gaidar's story 'The Blue Cup' [Golubaia chashka, 1935], which tells about a happy summer's day she spends with her father while her mother, Marusia, is meeting an old friend who serves as a fighter pilot.

The circular structure of time and space enhances the closed system of the film's narrative: there is no way out, either in time or space: the characters are entrapped. Outside the capital reigns the vastness of the Russian countryside; yet here too, enclosures dominate: the garden of the dacha is surrounded by a fence, and Nadia is forbidden to open the gate. Outside the garden, in the street, potential dangers lurk: the tanks, the black limousine, the evacuation exercise. The enclosure represents simultaneously entrapment and security.

Orientation and disorientation

The interior of the dacha offers a security that cannot be found outside: inside the dacha everything is where it belongs, photographs on the wall and towels in the drawer (Mitia still finds them after ten years' absence), while there are no directions beyond the fence of the dacha: the countryside is unmapped territory. Liuba is insecure when she is asked which village this is. The truck driver is disorientated and gets nowhere with his request for directions; moreover, the address he has been given was in the shirt that his wife unfortunately washed, and the letters have been obliterated. In the same way, many people would be 'washed away' or 'effaced' (*stertye*) during the purges. Furthermore, he has no map. He relies on others, not upon himself, to find the way, but nobody provides a definitive answer or a direction to follow: he is told only that it is 'not that way' (horseman), 'not here' (Liuba); later he is told to drive away from the construction site and to move out of the field. In fact, he is moving in circles. Only Kotov begins to provide a solution by suggesting a place 'Nagorie': the name signifies the top of the hill, a location with a view and a perspective from which he might be able to see his way, rather than implying danger (of sunburn); here the driver becomes a witness to Kotov's being beaten up, and he is shot.

The episode with the truck driver who has lost his way adds an absurd dimension to the film's narrative. This episode was inspired by an incident while Mikhalkov was shooting *Oblomov*, when the driver of the film team asked local people for directions and returned to the car with a bruised face. 'The driver is a metaphor for Russia that searches for its path, and everybody points her in different directions.'[6]

While the truck driver is blundering around the countryside, seeking to find his way on a vertical plane, the balloon is built to go upward into the air: it is designed to conquer space and offer an aerial view (as do the aeroplanes that Kotov hails in the fields as beautiful constructions that do not ruin the fields). Furthermore, it is a dirigible, a

4. The balloon construction site

balloon that does not float according to the forces of nature, but has an engine that allows for it to be steered in one direction: upwards. The dirigible fits fully into the concept of the conquest of space and territory so common in Stalinist culture,[7] whilst it is at the same time more ephemeral than an aeroplane. Inflated at first, a balloon will eventually crumple on descent.

Orientation, direction, and order are of significance in this new world outside the safety of the dacha. Kotov reminds Kirik to maintain order. Nadia longs for discipline when she expresses her wish to become a pioneer, so that she will also 'get up at the bugle's call, swim at the whistle's blast...' which Mitia completes with 'march to the drum's beat, eat in time, and if you do all that well, you get buried to music'. The discipline and uniformity that is desirable for Nadia only elucidates a cynical and mocking comment from Mitia. His belief in the system he works for is not just shattered, but entirely broken.

Contrasts and oppositions

In terms of structure *Burnt by the Sun* draws mainly on diametrical oppositions and contrasting principles. The film contrasts Moscow and the dacha, urban and rural life. It juxtaposes the idyllic setting at the dacha with its Chekhovian characters with the grey-and-red dominated picture of Moscow. The summer scenes of the main body of the film are contrasted with a brief glimpse of the winter season when Kotov and Marusia dance a tango at the pavilion as the film titles are shown. Classical music, arias from Italian operas, are opposed to Soviet march music. Western and Eastern traditions conflict: Kotov prefers the wooden bathhouse to a civilized bathroom; Mitia's tap-dance performance is answered by a Russian step-dance performance from Kotov; the Francophone family excludes Kotov who speaks no French. The individual games of tennis and croquet played before the Revolution are replaced by the collective (and more 'proletarian') game of football. The inside of the dacha is formed by a wooden interior with many photographs on the walls and rattan furniture, very much in a turn-of-the-century tradition; it is juxtaposed to the Soviet reality of marches and pioneers outside. A second, parallel, political reality impinges upon the idyll with the arrival of the tanks in the fields; the pioneers who march in honour of Stalin and who congratulate Kotov; the gas attack evacuation practice; and the scenes at the construction site where a dirigible is being built to raise Stalin's banner into the sky.

5. The pioneers' demonstration. They carry a portrait of Stalin

Temporally, the past and present are juxtaposed: the recollections of the past and the action in the present, the pre-Revolutionary dacha setting and the Revolutionary present. The world of children and pioneers, who look into the bright future, contrasts with the view into the past offered by the older generation.

These diametrical oppositions represent two worlds, each with a different pace of life, which conflict with each other: the frantic horseman interrupts Kotov's leisurely Sunday bath; the tanks shatter the peace in the fields and threaten the harvest; Mitia disturbs Marusia in her life from which he has been effaced; the truck interferes with the tranquillity of the village, of the peasant and of the construction site; the black limousine penetrates into the periphery like an envoy from the capital; and the evacuation exercise prevents relaxation at the beach.

These opposing principles serve to support the main contrast of the film: the theme of the marriage between the old Russian intelligentsia (Marusia) and the Revolutionary system (Kotov). The issue of whether this marriage works and whether the two systems are compatible is addressed: the marriage is based on lies (Kotov never confessed his

6. Nadia behind the gate that surrounds the dacha

involvement in sending Mitia away), and held together by Marusia's attempt to forget the past. The alliance survives, mainly because of the energy and (sexual) power of the Revolutionary, Kotov. It survives, however, only in a place that eclipses Soviet reality and continues with past traditions. The dacha is an artificial environment, out of space and out of time. Mitia is introduced to the viewer in terms of real time (for him time is indicated by the radio), and real space (Moscow). This reality destroys the illusion of a past life in a house protected from the outside world by gates and fences.

Duplicities: puns and *double-entendres*
The binary principle is also echoed in the duplicity and *double-entendres* which run throughout the film. The Soviet period was characterized not only by the renaming of places in honour of great Revolutionaries, but also by a plethora of acronyms, ranging from NKVD and KGB to the name of the country itself, USSR. This trend is mocked in the film by two acronyms: KhLAM, the name of the village of 'painters, writers, artists and musicians' (*poselok KHudozhnikov, Literatorov, Artistov i Muzykantov*) translates, when read as a proper word, as 'trash'; and

the name for the Civil Defence unit (*GRazhdanskaia OBorona*) is shortened to GROB, meaning 'coffin'.

Characters are rather playful with language, too: returning from the swim and the conversation with Mitia about the happy past, Marusia pretends to be 'injured' for the sake of the evacuation exercise, which has the benefit of her being carried away on a stretcher. Mitia emerges from the water behind her and claims to be 'dead'; yet as such he will not be carried away. The adjectives they choose reflect their emotional states: Marusia is hurt, her old wounds are uncovered because of the meeting with Mitia whom she had tried to forget; Mitia is 'effaced', annihilated, and emotionally dead.

Kotov's use of language differs from the family jargon used by the Golovins. His expression 'to put up a melon' (*vstavit' arbuz*), meaning 'to be caught up in a situation', is deliberately misunderstood by Vsevolod, who comments that this is the wrong season for melons. When Mitia repeats Boris Golovin's last words, 'trains with geese', Kotov cannot understand the significance of the phrase and replies instead on the level of recipes for the cooking of geese. Mitia identifies himself as part of the family by using their jargon: when he arrives, he greets everybody with a key phrase he remembers. Only Kotov is not greeted with a phrase, but instead Mitia reminds him of his telephone extension from the days when Kotov worked for the secret service. Mitia belongs there, Kotov does not. The Golovins (including Mitia), do not speak the same language as Kotov. Whilst the Golovins talk about the past, Kotov is interested in the future.

Past and future

In *Burnt by the Sun,* there are three generations that link the pre-Revolutionary past to the present: the fathers whose lifestyle of the past is dying out (Boris Konstantinovich); the children of the present times (Kotov, Mitia, Marusia); and the future generation represented by Nadia. The absence and presence of parents is an important feature: Mitia's parents have died during the Civil War, but he had been almost adopted by Marusia's father a long time ago. He is looked after by his tutor Philippe. Stalin is a father-figure to Mitia: when Stalin appears as an all-powerful pagan god, rising (on the banner attached to the balloon) as the sun is setting,[8] it becomes clear that he is a father-surrogate to Mitia who has no other family ties. Marusia's parents are educated and her family belongs to the intelligentsia. Kotov stays at

7. Vsevolod Konstantinovich (Viacheslav Tikhonov) reading the 'Pravda' newspaper

their dacha, although he shares neither their background nor their cultural tastes. Mitia has no children, while Marusia and Kotov have a daughter. Nadia's belief in the system and in the Soviet ideal is never shattered: she greets the pioneers in a professional, military manner; Kotov strengthens her enthusiasm, telling her about Soviet power which builds such flat roads that her heels will remain soft and rosy; she is not afraid of the men in the car, she even sits at the wheel when they leave with Kotov and returns to the dacha humming the title song.

The function of remembering the past is important within the narrative of the film rather than within its structure. In the atmosphere of the dacha Marusia's family reminisce about pre-Revolutionary times, a life enriched by traditions and values, by culture (music, dance, plays), which returns to the dacha with Mitia, and from which Kotov is excluded: he has no education and belongs to the new order. Mitia belongs culturally and socially with Marusia's family, but he has been alienated from it by Kotov, who recruited him for the secret service. Now he brings pre-Revolutionary activities back and excludes Kotov, who starts the meal alone as he is unable to dance the cancan. The political past forms the subject of a brief conversation during the football match, when Kotov reminds Mitia of the facts as he remembers them: Mitia was an officer for the Whites before becoming a secret agent for the OGPU in 1923 so that he could return from emigration. Mitia obediently rewrites Kotov's past for the confession he would soon make to the NKVD: that Kotov had been a German spy since 1920, and worked for the Japanese since 1923.

The past is, on the one hand, a happy memory; on the other it is part of history to be rewritten according to the dominant perspective

8. Nadia (Nadia Mikhalkova) saluting in front of the rising banner

on the political past at any given time. As such, personal memory is subordinated to political history.

Personal and political

Mitia's decisions are made for personal reasons, whereas Kotov is a military man whose personal life comes second to duty. The axis of the plot, however, is not the issue of Mitia wishing to destroy the world to which he no longer belongs; instead, he aims to annihilate Kotov's attempt to coexist in two worlds, something Mitia has not managed to do.

The film separates and intertwines the political and the personal: Mitia is politically successful, but his personal life has failed. Kotov has personal happiness and political power, and he loses both. Mitia commits suicide when he realizes the potential permanence of personal happiness as opposed to the transience of political success. The film underlines the personal dimension of the characters' conduct rather than their civic courage in sacrificing their personal life for a political cause.

Mitia has finished with his life and leaves it to chance (Russian roulette) whether he fulfils this assignment or not; if he does not arrest Kotov, then somebody else will. The system is permanent and indestructible. Mitia lost his personal happiness a long time ago, when he was recruited and left the country; it was then that he placed the political (illusion) before the personal (reality).

Choice and force

Kotov says that there is always a choice, like in the Russian fairy tale where there are three paths: standing at the crossroads, the character has to decide which way to go. Kotov has made a choice, but now he has no choice any more: he has to leave, just as Mitia had to leave then, ten years ago. Both Kotov and Mitia act for the sake of others (Marusia) and wish to protect the world of the past.

Mitia argues that he was forced to join the secret service and there was no choice ('I was forced'). Kotov has courage and power, enjoying 'paternal' protection from Stalin, and the knowledge of Stalin's direct line and the photographs testify to his status. Once he realizes that a change has taken place and Stalin is now a protector and father-figure for Mitia, he cries like a child disappointed by his parent and deprived of paternal love. The phrase he used to reproach

Mitia, 'there is always a choice', tragically proves wrong: there is no choice for Kotov.

The film raises the question of where the borderline lies between victim and oppressor, between the victim Kotov and the victim Mitia. Although one might argue at first sight that there is a crude dividing line between the positive hero Kotov and the offender and destroyer Mitia, between Kotov's Soviet heroism and Mitia's Western decadence, the film is much more complex than that: in Mitia's fairy tale Kotov is the ogre and the evil-doer. It depends, then, on one's point of view. The fireball symbolically points to the fact that Mitia died a long time ago when he lost his love, Marusia. Indeed, he tried to kill himself minutes before accepting the assignment to arrest Kotov. He knows that, without love, he is spiritually dead. In that sense, Kotov is a mere executor of the political will of Stalin, and acts under the illusion of having control (believing to the end that he can still rely on Stalin's support); Mitia, by contrast, has preserved his integrity: he acts, aware of the fact that he is a mere arm of power, an executor, an actor.

In *Burnt by the Sun* memory determines the action of the present: it is fixed, clear and precise. However, memory is personal: Kotov remembers different things about Mitia than the latter does. For Kotov, Mitia had a choice, whereas in Mitia's memory there was no choice. The accuracy of memory is thus undermined, and memory is shown to be individual rather than collective. Mitia is seen as a victim of personal circumstances that compel him to political activity. In a sense, Kotov can be viewed as a victim of Mitia's personal revenge rather than of the system (Kotov loses a father, while Mitia wins a father). Yet appearances are deceptive, the reality hidden under the inversion built by the narrative is that both are entrapped by the personal choices they have made in the past (Kotov admits in the car that he has made mistakes in the past). Kotov is a military man, and the tears he sheds in the car are over the loss of his political family rather than of Nadia and Marusia: after all, for him the political always comes first. History is seen as a conglomerate of personal (rather than political) decisions, and as such history is, retrospectively, man-made. It can be forged by man whose memory of the past is always subjective and selective, but this applies only to the past. In the present, history is not an active force but a passive construct that forces man into action, inducing him to react rather than act. The only demonstration of integrity lies in the acceptance of the fact that people in the 1930s were executors of Stalin's will.

Characters and Relationships

The triangle: Mitia

The main line of the character relationships is built on the duality that lies in the confrontation between Mitia and Kotov, rivals for Marusia's affection. Mitia returns to the house of the woman he loves, yet he peppers the conversation with constant reminders of her not as a young girl, but as a child. Mitia remembers how Marusia held his finger as a two-month old baby, how Boris Konstantinovich used to tell his wife to 'wipe Marusia's buttocks', while the recollection of their visit to the Bolshoi with Marusia aged six is restricted to the episode where Marusia had to go to the toilet: Mitia took her to the gents, where Rachmaninov mistook her for a boy in a dress. These are not the things that Marusia might want to be reminded of, and moreover they do not refer to their relationship as adults. Mitia is clearly indicating here to everybody around, including Kotov, that he is not there to claim Marusia back. Kotov is so certain of his power over Marusia that he has no qualms about leaving them alone, yet when they have left the beach he does become worried. Mitia even hits Kirik in the face when the latter suggests that he might rekindle the affair with Marusia. Mitia also ensures that everybody (except for Kirik) is under the illusion that he is married with three children, another safeguard against a potential renewal of the relationship with Marusia and against the impression of rivalry with Kotov. Mitia acts in a way to protect Marusia who is understandably shaken up in her artificially built and carefully created emotional security when he arrives (she drinks the water intended for Mitia, and she hastens to leave the room at the first opportunity).

Mitia is equally careful in the presence of the family: he gives no indication that he has come to arrest Kotov. The happy and pre-Revolutionary world of the *dachniki* is not shattered by his arrival; on the contrary, he brings back the atmosphere of the old days with his tap-dance and the music he plays on the piano. He is very playful with Nadia and relates extremely well to her, despite the fact that he has no children. Yet he recognizes in the six-year-old Nadia the girl Marusia, when aged six, the little girl he took to the Bolshoi Theatre and whom he taught to play the piano. Therefore his first recollection is of Marusia at the theatre with him, while he later repeats several times that Nadia is now the same age that Marusia then was. His relation to the little girl Marusia explains not only his experience of handling children, but also why he is so fond of Nadia. In fact, he receives from Nadia the attention he got from the little Marusia, but which he no longer attracts from the woman who is now Kotov's wife. Nadia is a substitute for Marusia. Indeed, Nadia and Marusia are very much alike: Marusia was mistaken for a boy when she was led to the gents at the Bolshoi theatre by her chaperone Mitia; Nadia is told off for jumping through the window like a boy.

Mitia's 'performance' underlines that he is playing a role, executing somebody else's plan. Just for one day he is the charming boy Mitia again, who took the hearts of Marusia's family by storm, the talented musician and entertainer. It is the only way he can go back into the past: masked as a clown. In reality, and he knows it perfectly well, he is a commanding officer of the NKVD with a special assignment. Here he does not fool around: Kotov understands in a second on the staircase what he has come for, and Mitia never forgets his task: he watches

9. Mitia (Oleg Menshikov) at the beach

Kotov carefully when he fetches the ball that has flown into the woods; he makes sure Kotov will sit in the back of the car rather than at the front with Nadia; and he loses all his capacity to entertain, even to speak, once they leave the dacha.

Mitia may be a clown and an actor in his interpretation of his role at the dacha, but he is also protective towards others, for example towards his tutor Philippe, although this may not appear at first sight to be the case: Mitia casually throws the coat at Philippe, who has been waiting until the early hours of the morning for Mitia to return; he orders Philippe to turn off the light and switch on the radio, and spends the rest of the scene correcting Philippe's pronunciation, having asked him to speak Russian. In fact, he is trying to protect Philippe, a foreigner in the Soviet state, with his insistence on speaking Russian. The Bolsheviks certainly speak no French (Kotov), a language associated with the bourgeoisie and the intelligentsia, while French was the language spoken by the aristocracy in nineteenth-century Russia. Although, according to the scenario, Philippe is in the flat in the final scene, we do not see him at the end of the film; he may already have disappeared.

Mitia protects others, too: according to the scenario he notices the

10. Mitia (Oleg Menshikov) comtemplating suicide

fireball and leads it away from the house in order to avert damage and harm from the people in the room. Indeed, Mitia is over-protective, but unlucky himself: in the scene at the beach he watches Kotov take off his shoes while standing next to a broken bottle; Kotov's feet miss the glass by an inch. Later Nadia runs to her father and Mitia stops her, worried that she may step on the glass, but Nadia has already run past it, unharmed. He then picks up the glass and throws it out of the way. After the swim he follows Marusia back to the beach and, trying to claim a stretcher as a 'killed' man, he is told that the Civil Defence Unit carries no dead bodies. At this point, he steps on to the very same glass he had removed earlier and cuts his foot: he is now injured and genuinely needs a stretcher. Mitia is injured by the item that he had identified as a potential danger: Kotov and Nadia remain unharmed, not even noticing the danger, while he is aware of it and still cuts himself. This small episode epitomizes the positions of Kotov and Mitia: Mitia is aware of the danger, and will eventually become a victim of the system himself, he will 'get burned'; Kotov is blissfully oblivious of the danger, and this time he goes unharmed. Kotov has, so far, escaped the danger that is lurking. Kotov is the lucky one: married to Marusia with a lovely daughter, a successful military leader; Mitia is the 'unlucky' one, with neither personal nor professional fulfilment.

While Kotov combines the world of the present with that of the past, the harmony of Marusia's family life with his military career, Mitia never succeeded in getting a share of both. Yet this is what he longed for all the time: to side with the Whites and to stay in Russia; to return to Russia with the help of the secret service and not continue to work for it; to marry Marusia despite his political past. His wish to have everything ultimately means compromise, and this is what he cannot reach. This dilemma is reflected in an everyday banality: in his reply to Nadia's question whether he wants 'tea with jam' or 'coffee with milk' Mitia says he would like 'coffee with jam'. As a result, he gets neither; worse still, he does not even get the glass of water he had asked for from Marusia.

The triangle: Kotov

Kotov is a man of great power and authority: military (tanks), sexual (Marusia), paternal (Nadia), social (bathers) and political (pioneers). He is kind and just: he gives the lieutenant a chance to recognize him, and checks that Mitia is all right after having hit him in the face during the football match. He believes in the ideals he has fought for: the building of socialism means flat roads to keep Nadia's heels rosy, aeroplanes to keep control without damage to the fields. His pursuit of physical exercise also reflects the obsession with the body characteristic of Stalinist culture, where the muscular bodies of the working class are the ultimate model for man's fitness to help build communism. Incidentally, only Kotov and Nadia seem to be interested in food, since they are the only characters who are seen eating in the film (Nadia eats bread with jam, Kotov the soup); the others presumably also have lunch, but this is not captured on camera. Kotov is a man of action who has little time for long explanations.

Kotov has fought on the side of the Bolsheviks against the White Army, and later became a divisional commander in the Red Army. He has at his disposal a car, a state dacha with security (he suggests to Marusia that they move there to avoid intrusions from the past, such as Mitia, and from outsiders, such as the horseman calling him into the fields), and he is widely respected (his portraits decorate many institutions). He tries to fit into Marusia's world, yet he still prefers the *bania* to the bathroom. He wears a white suit just like everybody else (only the NKVD officers wear grey), and modifies the family traditions slightly to make them more 'Soviet': he replaces croquet and tennis with football. He is excluded, though, from the cancan performed before lunch because he does not know the steps or the French language. Kotov tries to bridge the two worlds, to find compromises. Kotov is the first to break the awkward silence when everybody in the room is embarrassed about Mitia's attitude to Marusia in the presence of Kotov. Kotov invites everybody to go to the beach, where the clan breaks up into smaller parties.

Kotov believes that Mitia has come for personal revenge, whereas Mitia is a political executive. The world has changed: Mitia never dreamt he would find the world of Marusia's family intact, while Kotov believes that the world of the 1920s, when he rose to the top of the political structures, will be permanent. In fact, neither world is: Marusia's world will be annihilated by the system, while Kotov's world will be profoundly altered by the end of the film; a world where he believed himself to be in control, but is just as replaceable as everybody else, except for the Great Leader. Mitia at least knows that he is an executive, an actor, a puppet.

11. Kotov (Nikita Mikhalkov) introducing himself to the lieutenant (Evgeni Mironov)

Mitia believed in the system when he trusted the OGPU in their promise to repatriate him and then let him off the hook. A naive belief, perhaps, but such naiveté was common among Russian *émigré* circles in Europe in the 1920s. Kotov, in the meantime, took everything Mitia had longed for and betrayed him. Kotov claims that his actions were always motivated by a sense of duty for his country, whereas Mitia acted out of fear. Yet Mitia acted in defence of that pre-Revolutionary world in which Kotov now lives, like a parasite, with a beautiful and intelligent wife and a lovely child.

Kotov and Mitia differ in their views on choice and responsibility: Mitia claims that a choice between life and death is no choice; Kotov says there is always a choice. Of course, he is right, but the question remains – a choice between what and at what cost? Kotov and Mitia, in fact, respond in the same way to the 'choice': Mitia left the country without telling Marusia that he was acting on NKVD orders to protect her family, but – and here he is honest – also because he also wanted to live. Mitia does not pretend that he acted just out of a concern for others. Kotov, too, does not want anyone to know that he will be arrested in order not to upset the peace in the house. For both, incidentally, the choice is between life and death.

Kotov has something to live for in the ideal and perfect construction of the future. Mitia has no sense in his life. Kotov's life is taken, Mitia takes his own. He puts an end to being used for further tasks (the phone keeps ringing with possibly more special assignments while he lies in the bath). He knows that he is an arm of the system, and he makes a choice: to put an end to it. Kotov makes no choice in the present: he has chosen, once and for all time, to trust Stalin; now *he* makes the choices. Mitia is only an executive: if he does not carry out the arrest, somebody else will. Kotov, on the contrary, is used to giving orders. Kotov has made choices in the past, and so has Mitia. Some of Mitia's choices were not real choices, but questions of life and death, questions of the preservation of a way of life (with him as a part or not). Mitia betrayed those who fought with him, placing everything at stake in order to return to the world (of the past) to which he belonged. Yet he lost the game with the secret service, remaining on its

12. Kotov (Nikita Mikhalkov) with Marusia (Ingeborga Dapkunaite) and Mokhova (Svetlana Kriuchkova)

payroll. Mitia is a loser, he is doomed to defeat: he has lost the war, love, life.

Mitia twice recalls Boris Konstantinovich's last words: all that remained after a long life was the vision of trains with geese, a phrase taken from Chekhov's dying father. Mitia repeats these words to Marusia and Kotov, muttering them more to himself: that is all that will remain of this world, too: the insignificant image of geese being carried on trains. On the one hand, geese cackle, and this could be read as echoing the response of the intelligentsia to the Revolution by talking rather than acting. But geese are usually eaten (especially on holidays); Kotov's response to Mitia's remark reflects this: he remembers geese stuffed with apples.

Mitia knows that he has lost the game, and lost love. The absence of love alluded to in the title song defines the theme of the film: the absence of love is the reason for Mitia acting as he does. The motivation for actions is personal (nothing indicates that Mitia justifies his action by thinking that if he were to refuse, somebody else would act) and therefore guilt and responsibility lie with the individual.

The triangle: Marusia

Apart from the relationship between Kotov and Mitia other characters serve to bring out additional features and contrasts in that polar opposition. Marusia admires Kotov's military and sexual power, but is insecure when Mitia arrives. Although I would suggest that she knows that he is back in Russia (she received a letter on the morning of that day), she has to be 'taken' physically by Kotov to be convinced that she 'belongs' to him.

Her relationship with Mitia is one based on childhood recollections: Marusia and Mitia greet and say farewell by a gesture of piling up their hands, alluding to the past they share. Their relationship seems to have stagnated on the level of the feelings of an upset teenager: she spent her first night with Mitia after she had run away, having discovered that her mother was having an affair with Kirik only a month after her father's death. Mitia recalls Hamlet's lines: 'Within a month / Ere yet the salt of most unrighteous tears / Had left the flushing in her galled eyes, / She married...' with which Hamlet comments on Gertrude's premature and predatory marriage to Claudius.[9] Mitia draws a parallel between Gertrude and Olga Nikolaevna, with himself assuming the part of Hamlet, who will deliberately seek death while his love for

13. Mitia (Oleg Menshikov) and Marusia (Ingeborga Dapkunaite) pile up their hands as a gesture of farewell

14. Marusia (Ingeborga Dapkunaite) at the beach

15. Mitia (Oleg Menshikov) recalling his love for Marusia and reciting from *Hamlet*

Ophelia has no future and Ophelia's happiness is doomed. Mitia adopts the role of Hamlet, the betrayed son, who is to die while his beloved Ophelia (Marusia) will drown: Marusia will be arrested shortly after Kotov.

Mitia asks for a glass of water, which Marusia fetches for him in an attempt to get away and avoid him. She runs the tap of the samovar until the water overflows, while she gazes absent-mindedly into the void. She then drinks the glass in one gulp and takes the empty glass into the room, tapping her nails on the edge. Mitia never gets the water he asked for, but Marusia takes it away from him: she withholds the essence of life from him. Marusia fails to respond directly both to Mitia's tale and to his recollections of the first night they spent together in the boathouse. Instead, in both instances, she runs away. She wants no disturbance in her world, and actively encourages him to leave once Kotov has manifested his power over her. Marusia wants to be taken by a winner rather than a loser.

Nadia, or Hope

Nadia is a bright and clever girl who comments on the behaviour of adults with a certain lack of respect, often found in an only child. Kirik drinks, and she smells his breath; she also tells her father off for having drunk and not eaten anything to cover the smell of alcohol. She pokes her finger into the jam, although she knows that this is bad manners, and she disrespectfully dishevels Vsevolod Konstantinovich's hair; she even teases one of the the NKVD officers with her question whether he has been to the zoo. After the affirmative answer, she promptly asks why he ran away from there and whether he was not fed well. Nadia wants to be a pioneer, and loves the order and discipline of the pioneers. She also shows a great deal of compassion when she consoles Mokhova over the medicines, and asks the magician-doctor Mitia to come into the house so that he can attend to her. Nadia immediately likes Mitia, confiding in him and asking him into the house.

Nadia's typical gesture – which her father loves – is that of a 'platypus': she pulls up her upper lip to make it meet her nose. A duckbilled platypus is a strange hybrid of an animal that lays eggs but suckles its young, a mixture of bird and mammal. Nadia too, is a cross-breed between the old and new order, the pre-Revolutionary world and that of the new Soviet order. Her name Nadia is the short form for Nadezhda, meaning 'hope' – for the coexistence of two worlds or the establishment of a Soviet paradise?

Other characters

Mokhova cries bitterly over the lost medicine; she is a spinster who swallows medicine indiscriminately and whose only worry is that everybody tries to grab her breasts. She is upset once her medicine has been thrown away, and even more so when Mitia discovers a toffee he hid ten years ago – a proof that she does not dust. She is portrayed as good-natured and caring, looking after both Nadia (whose doll she dragged to the beach) and Kotov (whom she finds alone at the table and takes action by calling everybody to lunch in the language he does not speak: French). Her name, derived from the word 'moss', reflects both her unattractiveness and the quality of a cushion.

Kirik is a womanizer, who constantly borrows money and is tipsy most of the time. He teaches the budgerigars silly phrases and makes a pass at Liuba, while none of his actions is ever serious. In fact, when Kotov suspects he is making love to Liuba in the room from which the sound of a squeaking bed and heavy breathing can be

16. Mokhova (Svetlana Kriuchkova) in her room, with drawings of hands and naked female figures pinned to the wall.

17. Kirik (Vladimir Ilyin)

heard, he is innocently in the same room with her pumping up a ball. Kirik also uses a mask, that of a womanizer-*cum*-alcoholic, in order to cope with the realities of life, in which he is in charge of film screenings in a local sanatorium. His name suggests 'drinking buddy' (*kiriat* means 'to booze'). He sees through Kotov and understands Mitia, but there is nothing he could usefully do. So he too, like Mitia, adopts a mask, fools around and pretends. This is why Mitia tells Kirik the truth: that he is not married and works for the NKVD. But he was only joking...

Liuba is an excellent sparring partner for Kirik, yet she is also full of admiration for Kotov, gaping at him. She is caricatured as a pseudo-intellectual who would like to be part of the intelligentsia, but admires the Soviet system.

Vsevolod Konstantinovich is a professor of Roman Law; his words are carefully monitored by Olga Nikolaevna, who is aware of the potential for dispute between him and Kotov. Olga Nikolaevna herself is a scheming and manipulative woman, controlling Kirik, with whom she had an affair while her husband was still alive. She is selfish and preoccupied with her own beauty: as Kotov departs, she asks him to bring some cosmetics from the city.

Images and Mirror-images

The polarity between the two worlds contrasted in the ideas held by Kotov and Mitia and reflected both in the structural pattern and the character relationships also dominates the images used in the film. Water, whose surface reflects; water, which is used to clear the ground; the colour contrast of red and white; the use of mirrors and disguises (masks and fairy tales) to invert reality form the underlying dual principle of the film's visual language.

Water

The imagery used in *Burnt by the Sun* is focused on the absence and presence of water. During Mitia's stay at the dacha, several claps of thunder are audible in the background, but there is no rain: the standard image for the Revolution as a cleansing force is rejected.

Mitia elaborately washes his face twice in the film: when he returns to the Moscow flat in the morning, and when he arrives at the dacha

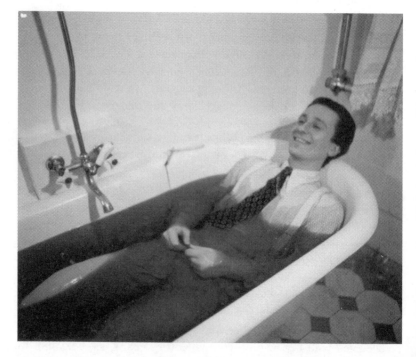

18. Mitia (Oleg Menshikov) in the bathtub, having slit his wrists

having removed his beard and moustache; it seems as though he is washing his face to wipe it clean for his next mask. Kotov avoids contact with water: while Mitia uses the bathroom sink, Kotov prefers the *bania* (steam bathhouse). Kotov takes Nadia out in a boat *on* the river, while Marusia and Mitia swim *in* the river. In fact, Mitia dives for quite a long time, and the conversation he has with Marusia on the other side of the river reveals his true self: Marusia has everything, while he has nothing. Mitia remembers the happiness of the past in this conversation with Marusia and confesses to the absence of love in his life, a theme underlined by the title song: 'The weary sun gently bid farewell to the sea, and at this hour you confessed that there is no love...'.

Mitia's suicide in the final scene is again associated with water: in his white clothes he is lying in a bathtub filled with water, having cut his wrists, while his blood is staining the water red. His death links him to Marusia, who had tried to cut her wrists, but did not know that 'one has to do it in water'. He takes his life in the way Marusia had wanted to take hers when he left her.

Colours

In this final scene of Mitia's suicide the camera moves from the bathtub to a Kremlin tower decorated with a red star, also shown in the first frame of the film.

The colour symbolism extends to costumes and clothing: the *dachniki* are all in white, seated on their rattan furniture. Their white dress (a reference also to the 'White' army) is contrasted to the grey of the NKVD officers' suits and of the grey concrete structure of the House on the Embankment, symbolizing power; Kotov's uniform in which he leaves is also grey. The balloon which pulls up Stalin's portrait is of a silvery grey. The colour black only features on the car which comes to take Kotov and Mitia back to Moscow. A tint of blue sometimes complements the colour range of the costumes (Mitia's shirt is striped white and blue, Vsevolod Konstantinovich's collar has a blue edge, Olga Nikolaevna wears a bright blue top and Mokhova's dress is light blue) extending the colour range to that of the Russian flag. Nature shots usually show the dark green of the woods, a bright blue sky and the intense yellow of the fields.

The colour red is associated with the Soviet way of life: the pioneers' ties, the flags on the trumpets, the flags at the beach and in the street, the banners on the House on the Embankment and on the construction site of the dirigible, the stars on the Kremlin towers, but most importantly the banner with the portrait of Stalin that rises on the horizon at the end of the film. Red is the colour of the blood on Kotov's face and in Mitia's bath. It is implied here that the Soviet power represented by the colour red is the same as blood, and built on the blood of the people.

The fireball

Twice in the film a special effect is used: the fireball. 'What is the fireball? It is the Revolution. It is not by accident that at the beginning of the film the Frenchman Philippe reads a newspaper article about a fireball that destroys everybody in motion, who thrust themselves forward. But for me this explanation does not mean anything – it is rather for critics and students.... For me the fireball is an emotion that requires no explanation.'[10]

When Mitia tells the fairy tale about the past, the fireball emerges on the river, enters the house and makes the glass on a photograph burst before it leaves the house. The fireball ignites in collision with a falcon and eventually burns down one tree in the wood. This destruction of a bird and a single tree in the wood can be interpreted as the destruction of Mitia's life for the first time, when Marusia was taken away from him. The second fireball effect accompanies Mitia's physical destruction, his suicide. The fireball is red and can also be understood as a symbol for the Soviet system in an extension of the colour symbolism discussed above. In this reading the system destroys one single tree in an indiscriminate manner. The effect is symbolic and not integrated in the overall realism of the film.[11] It obtrudes as artificial, although it is reported in the newspaper article that Philippe reads at the beginning of the film. It is unreal in that nobody notices the fireball, nor the effect that it has on the picture (showing a happy family scene). According to the scenario Mitia noticed the fireball and prevented it from causing havoc and destruction inside the house, underlining once more his protective behaviour towards others.

Masks and carnival

Mitia appears as an old, blind man emerging from the pioneers marching past the dacha: he is a blank page on to which any history and any identity can be written. In order to win Nadia's heart he poses

19. Mitia (Oleg Menshikov) in the disguise of an old, blind man

as a magician; in order to gain entrance into the house he claims to be a doctor. He removes his carnival disguise, only to put on another mask; some time later he wears a gas mask. He is an entertainer, musician, dancer, story-teller, as well as a calculating NKVD officer who does his job. He pretends to be married with three children, yet he is a sad, lonely man. He can adopt any role, indeed needs to do so in order to give his life a meaning, at least temporarily. He recites the tunes he taught Marusia, repeats the steps he learnt in Paris, cites Hamlet, plays an invalid at the beach to be helped up by the fat lady asking him for the time, and 'performs' a dive into the river. His every movement is a calculated action, a performance. There is no other way for him to return to the past than by creating a carnival atmosphere that allows him to behave like a child and play all sorts of – forbidden – games. He needs to create masks for himself, rather than a person-ality; he lacks psychological depth and, burdened with his role, he cannot change or reveal his emotions.[12]

If Mitia is an actor who performs roles, Kotov is an image that cannot change. Mitia wrote this part for himself whereas Kotov is a portrait in a world replacing its idols. Stalin's portrait features in central episodes in the film: first on the façade of Mitia's house; then

on the shirts of the pioneers; later the camera shows a close up of one
of the photographs in the dacha: Stalin with Kotov. Stalin's portrait
finally rises on the balloon. Effigies of the Leader were displayed
everywhere in the 1930s. But Kotov's portraits are also displayed
everywhere, as several characters remark: Liuba has seen Kotov's
portrait at the university and is excited to see the man in person; the
lieutenant in command of the tanks also recognizes Kotov, but only
when he has put a cap on and posed in profile. He is so impressed
that he freezes with a huge smile of respect and honour, to the extent
that he even forgets his name ('Misha, no, sorry, Kolia'). The truck
driver also forgets his concern with Zagorianka when he sees Kotov in
the car. His curiosity costs him his life: when he asks Mitia after the
violent incident in the car whether this is really Kotov, he is shot. The
encounter with Kotov has a similar effect on people to the encounters
with Stalin portrayed in Soviet films of the 1930s and 1940s: recognition of the goal of socialism. Indeed, Kotov somewhat resembles
Stalin with his huge moustache. Again with a warning note Mitia tells
Marusia that images may soon collapse; and Kotov is only an image.
At the same time, the popularity of effigies of any other leader but

20. Mitia (Oleg Menshikov) watching the balloon rise

Stalin can be compared to the rivalry between Kirov and Stalin in 1934; a short time later Stalin instructed the NKVD to eliminate his rival.

Mitia's grin when he faces the portrait of the Great Leader rising on the dirigible inverts the moment of recognition that the sight of the Leader instigated in other films.[13] Mitia is about to light a cigarette, which he holds between his lips, while the match is between his fingers; he contracts and distorts his face to a huge grin: he has done the job, as the leader wanted. Mitia smokes *papirosy*, a sign of the bourgeoisie (Rachmaninov smoked them too), and keeps these in a silver cigarette case; both the case and the cigarettes are a remnant of a bourgeois lifestyle. As he walks back to the car, he spits out the cigarette: he has played his role, and there is no longer any need to pretend that he belongs to that world of the past.

Mirrors

The principle of opposition leads, on the one hand, to the theme of the interference of one world in another; on the other it offers the possibility of an inversion of the two worlds. Apart from the inversion of reality into a fairy tale there is a more mundane inversion of reality: in the mirror.

Mirrors prepare new 'images': Marusia first looks at Mitia – and herself – in the mirror. She fails to see his true mission, thinking he has come to claim her back. Mitia, on the other hand, looks at himself in the mirror when washing his face as if to find his next identity. Nadia uses the headlight of the car to make sure her hair and eyebrows look pretty, creating and polishing her image as a Soviet pioneer girl, before she speaks to the NKVD officers in the car.

Reflected (mirrored) images conceal the truth as much as visions are distorted: on the beach Mitia looks at Kotov through the broken end of a bottle, a perspective the camera does not capture: Mitia's view of Kotov differs from ours: he sees in him the traitor, the man he has to arrest, the sexual competitor, while objectively he is (still) the powerful military man and loving father.

In the final sequence of the film we see the ultimate function of the mirror as a substitute for reality: it reflects selected images only. The mirror of the dressing table among the furniture on the truck reflects the image of Stalin carried by the balloon. The monumental size of the image distracts from the real fact: the dead body of the driver

21. Nadia (Nadia Mikhalkova) by the car that has come to arrest her father

insufficiently covered by a tarpaulin among the furniture. This again echoes the preoccupation with a monumental building style during the Stalin period that created a façade behind which Stalin's crimes were hushed up, just as the Nazi crimes were concealed behind the grandiose Olympic Games in Berlin in 1936.

Mirror-images of fairy tale and reality

A fairy tale is reality beautified, the inversion of the reality on earth, seen in the light of cosmic transcendence.[14] Fairy tales almost always have a happy ending. When Mitia first appears, he is a 'Santa Claus' (*ded moroz*) – in the middle of the summer. He emerges from a group of marching pioneers who are singing the 'Aviators' March' (by Pavel German and Yuli Khait, 1920):

> We were born to make a fairy tale come true,
> To conquer the distances and space,
> Our minds made steel wings for our hands,
> And throbbing engines take the place of our hearts.

Ever higher, higher and higher
We aim the flight of our birds,
The tranquillity of our borders
Breathes in each propeller.[15]

The song anticipates the 1930s' call for a varnished and perfected
reality, while it also echoes two themes relevant to the film: the birds
that fly too high and get burnt by fireballs; and the theme of aeroplanes
that conquer territory. 'We are born to make a fairy tale come true' is
the premise upon which Mitia enters the house. Nadia's first question
for the magician from the country of the Maghreb, the country of
summer Santas, is whether the country is Soviet, and only her second
question is whether there are winter Santas as well:

– Are you the summer Santa?
– Yes, Nadia, I'm the wizard from the Maghreb.
– What's the Maghreb?
– The Maghreb is the land where the summer Santas live.
– In the USSR?
– Of course. All the summer Santas live in the USSR.
– And the winter ones?
– They do, too.

Although Mitia has entered the world of fairy tales, he speaks the truth:
he is from the country of the Maghreb, the Arab word for West. The
happy past is remembered in the form of a fairy tale narrated by Mitia,
about the boy Yatim who was taken on by the kind musician Sirob
who then had a daughter, Yasum; Yatim then had to fight in the war,
and when he returned Yasum had become a beautiful princess and
Yatim fell in love with her. But then an important man – whose name
he cannot remember – took Yasum away from him and sent Yatim
abroad.

Mitia inverts the names of the protagonists (Mitia and Musia, a
diminutive for Marusia, in itself a diminutive for Marina or Maria) to
Yatim and Yasum. Mitia's fairy tale lacks, however, the happy ending
that Nadia expects. The inversion of names also reflects the inversion
of worlds, of the old order for the new, and as such continues the
principle of oppositions and contrasts. Mitia's and Marusia's names, as
well as Nadia's, are marked on the glass panel by the door. Mitia

marks his height and age now, in the present, as Yatim, aged 37: he has changed his identity. Nadia understands the principle of fairy tales very well: she expects a happy ending, and when Yatim and Yasum do not marry she correctly assumes that the 'important man' must be an ogre. She also understands the principle of inversion of names and applies it to herself: she figures out that she would be Yadan in the story. But she does not decipher the inverted names of the fairy tale figures. Nadia transposes herself into fairy worlds, but does not transpose the fairy-tale world into reality. The principle advocated in the Soviet march does not work: we do not turn the fairy tale into reality, but make reality a fairy story, a myth, a lacquer box.

Mitia uses Nadia's dolls to illustrate his story. Earlier at the beach Nadia had rejected the doll as a toy for children, while she is a 'big girl', and given it to Mitia to play with. Mitia uses a small, naked doll for Yatim, and a tall, dressed doll for Yasum. The boy is naked, the girl dressed, an image repeated (off camera) when Mitia has finished playing the piano with a red gown on while his clothes are drying on the line; he throws the gown at Marusia, thus sitting naked and wearing a gas mask at the piano, and this causes Marusia to run away with hysterical laughter after throwing the dry clothes and shoes at him.

The past is narrated in the form of a tale, illustrated by puppets, or performed by Mitia wearing the mask of an old beggar. It is never spoken of in real terms, except for the scene between Kotov and Mitia during the football match, when facts are named; however, even these facts depend on the individual's memory, and as such history depends on subjective perception.

Kotov refers to Mitia as a bad story teller and later calls him Andersen. Two things are remarkable here: fairy tales are part of a folk and oral tradition, which was being assimilated in the 1930s for propaganda purposes. Fairy tales of the type of Gaidar,[16] with pioneer girls and Soviet realia, were favoured. Andersen, however, is a foreign fairy-tale writer (rather than a collector like his Russian counterpart, Afanasiev), which again points to Mitia's foreign influence and education.[17] For Mitia's fairy tale there is no happy ending. If that fairy tale is turned into reality it implies a bad ending of the story: for 'uncle' Mitia and the ogre Kotov. And a bad ending, by extension, of the dream of the pioneers who aspire ever higher.

Music

Diegetic music

In the arts, the year 1936 was noted for putting an end to the new wave of jazz music and for turning improvisation into conventional and well-rehearsed performances of the *estrada* (variety performance). Ballroom music and tangos were so popular that even Red Army officers were instructed how to dance, including General Voroshilov. The composition of Soviet marches to replace folk tunes (folklore being seen as a backward tendency) reached its peak in the 1930s.[18] Soviet music thus dominates the scenes associated with Kotov and the military: the pioneers parade to the 'Aviators' March'; they listen to Soviet marches at the beach; and the trumpet is appropriately the instrument associated with Kotov.

The tango 'The Weary Sun' ('Utomlennoe solntse'), along with the jazz compositions of the 1930s that are played on the radio for the football match, represents a compromise: such music was entertaining and popular, whilst it was also decadent in origin. Like the foxtrot in the 1920s, the tango would become unpopular with the authorities in the late thirties, while jazz music would be banned outright in part for its improvisational character. The tango is the song that is associated with Marusia and Kotov, with their love that bridges the two worlds of the military and the artistic intelligentsia, forming a link between the new and the old order. The tango is also a personal tune for Mitia, in that the text sums up his dilemma: it reflects the theme of lost love, and it is hummed by the substitute for his 'beloved', Nadia.

Utomlennoe solntse, / nezhno s morem proshchalos', / v etot chas ty priznalas', / chto net liubvi.
Mne nemnogo vzgrustilos', / bez toski, bez pechali, / v etot chas prozvuchali, / slova tvoi.
Rasstaemsia, ia ne budu zlit'sia, V etom vinovaty i ty i ia.

(The weary sun gently bade farewell to the sea, and at that hour you confessed that love had gone. I was a little sad. No melancholy or sadness resounded in your words at that hour. Let us part; I shall not be angry. You and I are both to blame.)

The song concludes on the note that both parties are to blame: Kotov and Mitia for the failure in their political lives, Marusia and Mitia for the failure of their love.

The other song of importance for the plot of the film is 'Evening Bells' ('Vechernii zvon'), based on a poem by Thomas Moore ('Those Evening Bells') and translated into Russian by Ivan Kozlov (1827). The song, which appears only in the Russian cut of the film, has become part of Russian folk lore. Its lines are about the memory of the past, the recollection of a happy youth, which has gone forever not to be seen again; it is the song of a man who is saying his last farewell to a happy past, and preparing to die, as does Mitia when he leaves the dacha to return to Moscow to end his life. The choir of the women is conducted by Mitia, and the song is an oratorio for him on his last visit to the house with which his happy past is connected.

> Those evening bells! those evening bells!
> How many a tale their music tells,
> Of youth, and home, and that sweet time,
> When last I heard their soothing chime.
>
> Those joyous hours are pass'd away;
> And many a heart, that then was gay,
> Within the tomb now darkly dwells,
> And hears no more those evening bells,
>
> And so 'twill be when I am gone;
> That tuneful peal will still ring on,
> While other bards shall walk these dells,
> And sing your praise, sweet evening bells!
>
> Thomas Moore

The *dachniki* sing this song in complete oblivion of the fact that Kotov will be executed, and their idyllic life will be destroyed within days. As such, the song is the most frightening sequence in the film: 'The most cruel episode in the film is the quiet, sweet, semi-romantic song of the old Chekhovian characters with which they accompany the car taking Kotov into non-existence. They see nothing. They think nothing. Choristers.'[19]

Non-diegetic music

The film music was specially composed by Eduard Artemiev, who had already collaborated with Mikhalkov on previous occasions. The non-diegetic music is scarce and unobtrusive, accompanying and acoustically uniting certain themes that are visually separated, such as the theme of 'Father and Daughter' in the scenes concerning Kotov and Nadia, or the theme of the 'Balloon Construction' for sequences at the construction site.

Sound

The soundtrack was recorded on location rather than recorded specially at the studio. This helps to create the impression that the characters do not attribute much importance to the words they say: words have, as in the Theatre of the Absurd, lost their function as devices which enable communication; rather, they serve to cover up events which remain unmentioned, or which are disguised in costumes and fairy tales.

The players

Mikhalkov himself chose to play the commander Kotov, thus casting himself in the role of a man who honestly believes in the system and becomes its victim. His daughter Nadia plays his daughter in the film, and he has commented that he took the part to help Nadia in the scenes between father and daughter. However, it is significant that Mikhalkov's charisma – as a successful film-maker and committed nationalist he is somewhat of a cult figure – immediately tips the viewer's sympathy towards Kotov, who therefore comes across much more as a victim than as a mixture of both loser and winner, victim and oppressor.

Ingeborga Dapkunaite is an internationally renowned actress from Lithuania. She has played many parts, mostly depicting modern, independent women (Katia in Valeri Todorovsky's *Katia Izmailova* [Podmoskovnye vechera, 1994], Kisulia in Petr Todorovsky's *Intergirl* [Interdevochka, 1989], Olga in Dmitri Meskhiev's *The Cynics* [Tsiniki, 1991]). She has also appeared as Harrer's wife in *Seven Years in Tibet* [USA, 1997] and in *Mission: Impossible* [USA, 1996]. In a sense, this role is slightly outside her usual range. As Marusia she never makes clear how much she knows and whom she loves the more, thus veiling her seemingly passive and receptive nature in secrecy.

Oleg Menshikov has risen to stardom, not least because of his part in this film. He has often played characters who need to forge a mask for themselves in order to create – artificially – some meaning in their lives: Andrei Pletnev in Alexander Khvan's *Diuba-Diuba* [1992], a scriptwriter who devises a plan to help his ex-girlfriend escape from prison, only to realize that she does not love him any more; Sasha Kostylin, the soldier in captivity in Sergei Bodrov's *The Prisoner of the Mountains* [Kavkazskii plennik, 1996], who has no family whilst inventing stories about his past. He has acted in a number of theatre productions both in Russia and abroad (Esenin in the London production *When She Danced* ... with Vanessa Redgrave), and most recently Chatsky in a Moscow production of Griboedov's *Woe from Wit* which he also directed. He has starred in Mikhalkov's *The Barber of Siberia* [Sibirskii tsiriulnik, 1998] in the role of the cadet Andrei Tolstoi, and in the role of the invalid Lyonia in Denis Evstigneev's *Mama* [1999].

Vladimir Ilyin (Kirik) is a comic actor who has mainly played supporting roles and is thus extremely suited for the part of the 'lover of sweet wines and young women'. Viacheslav Tikhonov (Vsevolod) is a veteran actor who has starred in films since 1948. He is best known for his role as Stirlitz in the classic Soviet spy-serial *Seventeen Moments of Spring* [17 mgnovenii vesny, 1973]. Inna Ulianova (Olga) works in both theatre and film, and her range of roles is largely 'Soviet'-type women, scheming, forceful and energetic. The part she plays implies that she is having an affair with the younger Kirik, an affair that started shortly after Boris had died. In that sense, she has compromised her moral values.

It is worth noting that many of Mikhalkov's actors are theatre actors, accustomed to 'performing' in the true sense of the word, rather than posing for the camera. Mikhalkov's interest lies in the psychological development of the character over the entire film rather than within episodes or individual frames. The choice of stage actors enabled Mikhalkov to hold long shots in order to capture the duration and seeming permanence of happiness in the countryside as opposed to cutting scenes on the editing table.

Notes

1 I am grateful to Richard Taylor for drawing my attention to this fact.
2 I am indebted to Anatoli Ermilov for this information.
3 Sergei Mikhalkov, 'Ia sluzhil gosudarstvu', interview with Irina Arzamastseva, *Kontinent* 96 (1998), pp. 342–57.

4   Nikita Mikhalkov, 'Rezhisser ne dolzhen dolgo nakhodit'sia pod obaia-
    niem svoei kartiny. Eto opasno', *Iskusstvo kino* 3 (1995), pp. 9–13; p. 12.
5   Yuri Trifonov, *Dom na naberezhnoi* (The House on the Embankment), in
    Sobranie sochinenii, vol. 2, Moscow, 1986.
6   Mikhalkov, 'Rezhisser ne dolzhen...', p. 12.
7   Katerina Clark, *Petersburg: Crucible of Cultural Revolution*, Cambridge MA,
    1995, and Vladimir Paperny, *Kul'tura dva*, Moscow, 1996.
8   A similar scene is described in Yuri Trifonov's uncompleted novel *Ischezno-
    venie* (Moscow, 1988), where a dirigible with Stalin's portrait floats over the
    nocturnal Moscow.
9   Hamlet, act I, scene 2, ll. 153–6.
10 Nikita Mikhalkov, 'Rezhisser ne dolzhen...', p. 12.
11 See Louis Menashe's review in *Cineaste*, XXI, 4 (1995), pp. 43–4.
12 For a full discussion of the elements of the game see Kulish's review trans-
    lated in this book.
13 Examples of such films where the encounter with Stalin (or a portrait)
    inspire belief in socialism can be found in many films of the 1930s and
    1940s, ranging from Aleksandrov's *The Circus* (1936) to Chiaureli's *The Fall
    of Berlin* (1949). See Richard Taylor, *Film Propaganda*, London, 1998.
14 Compare Andrei Siniavsky's study of *svet* in the fairy tale in *Ivan-durachok*
    (Ivan the Fool).
15 Pavel German, Yuli Khait, 'Aviators' March', 1920, translated in von
    Geldern and Stites, *Mass Culture in Soviet Russia*, Bloomington, 1995, pp.
    257–8.
16 Arkadi Gaidar (1904–41), writer of children's books, which became Soviet
    classics.
17 Hans Christian Andersen, writer of fairy tales; Alexander Afanasiev,
    collector of fairy tales.
18 Richard Stites, *Russian Popular Culture: Entertainment and Society since 1900*,
    Cambridge, 1992, chapters 2 and 3.
19 Alexander Arkhangelsky, 'Desnitsa i shuitsa N. S. Mikhalkova', *Iskusstvo
    kino* 3 (1995), pp 5–8; p. 5.

4. The Film and its Context

Reassessing the Past: The Stalin Period in Recent Cinema *b.s exploring e i*

Although Khrushchev in his 'Secret Speech' (1956) had addressed the terror and the injustice of the Stalin regime, open discussion of the Soviet past did not extend to areas of cultural life. The 'Thaw' in the arts (1956–64) primarily allowed the discussion of problems of contemporary life, whilst any reassessment of the past remained the privilege of the Party officials and those in charge of rehabilitation. Gorbachev's *glasnost* and *perestroika* of the late 1980s opened the closed chapters of Soviet history for reinterpretation, and thus had an enormous impact on the production and release of films and on the publication of literature dealing with Soviet history of the Stalin era. For the first time, the Stalin era was explicitly dealt with in many films, plays and novels; the newly available accessibility of archival material and documents relating to the period furthered this interest.

In the late 1980s the concern with the 1930s had been reflected in the form of an attempt to restore in the people's memory those pages of Soviet history that had been blotted out; artistically, this was expressed in the form of an appeal to remember the 1930s as the enormous human sacrifice in the struggle against fascism during the Second World War. In the 1990s the interest in the 1930s coincided with the active rewriting of the history of a state that had at that point collapsed: documents had been released, and history had been discussed openly, explicitly, and subjectively. Now it was time to consider the lessons to be drawn from the 1930s, to look for parallels in the quest of both decades, the 1930s and the 1990s, to define a new nationhood. Issues of individual choice and responsibility with regard to history and politics are also treated differently in films of the post-*perestroika* and the post-Soviet periods.

Stalin after *perestroika*

Tengiz Abuladze's *Repentance* [Pokaianie/Monanieba, 1984, release 1986] became a cult film of the 1980s. It was the first film to address the purges of the 1930s, even if it did so in a highly allegorical form. The film's poetic language and its complexity can partly be explained by the use of Aesopian language typical of authors treating 'forbidden' themes in the Brezhnev era, and by the school of Georgian film-makers traditionally using a more symbolic film language.

The film offers an utterly pessimistic perspective on the relationship between history and the individual and on the lack of a future for either victims or oppressors. Keti is decorating cakes at the beginning and the end of the film. Her childhood, which she remembers during the trial, and her present occupation are the only realities the film offers. Her resistance to terror (her exhumation of the dictator Aravidze's body, the consequent trial and her forgiveness) only happens in her imagination, while in reality she lacks the courage she wishes she might have. Keti does not take revenge in the reality in which she lives; her revenge takes place in her imagination. Forgiveness reigns in reality, not repentance. This Christian message informs the reply of the old woman asking for the way: any road will lead to the church; any path will eventually lead to God and He will pass the ultimate judgement. Abuladze does not condemn Keti, who in her imagination also clearly sees the outcome of her revenge: she will be silenced. Her inactivity is criticized and legitimized at the same time: her action could deprive Aravidze of his eternal rest; it could make the family suffer, but it would also commit Keti to a psychiatric clinic; it is legitimized on the religious level, leaving it for God to judge. Throughout the film Abuladze extensively draws on religious imagery (the demolition of the Church of Christ the Saviour, the confession to a 'priest', the burial of the dead), while Mikhalkov relies on the single image of Stalin as a pagan God.

Keti is a victim of a collective history in which individual action led to destruction. Keti's freedom, and her potential for activity, are crippled by the force of history. The only morality that remains intact lies in the church. Such escapism, or withdrawal to religion instead of political activity, would be rejected by film-makers in the 1990s: in Mikhalkov's *Burnt by the Sun* the road that in *Repentance* led to the church would lead to Moscow, representing both Mitia's and Kotov's death.

Repentance is timeless, without specific references to the 1930s; *Burnt by the Sun* is specific in time and place. While *Repentance* paralyses its characters in their imagination, many films of the 1990s dealing with Stalinist terror interpret the potential for activity in the 1930s as an illusion. Although *Burnt by the Sun* also uses a circular structure that offers no escape to the characters, they are doomed by the system rather than crippled by their own minds. Neither film-maker condemns his characters' actions. The theme of the memory of the past as collective or individual forms a common interest for Abuladze and Mikhalkov; both directors also show an interest in mirror images that distort reality. A significant difference, however, lies in the complete absence of the religious theme in Mikhalkov's film. While religion may have been a way out of the moral dilemma in the 1980s, it is no longer perceived as a solution worth advertising in the 1990s; rather, it is an escape from the real problem which lies not in the individual's conscience, but in his misapprehension of the system.

The second important film of the 1980s about Stalin's terror is Alexei German's *My Friend Ivan Lapshin* [Moi drug Ivan Lapshin, 1983, release 1985]. Lapshin is a police officer who fights a local gang of criminals and eventually shoots the leader of the gang. He carries out his duties with honesty and conviction, believing in the ideals of socialism. *Lapshin* is a realistic portrayal of ordinary everyday life, without any propaganda or illusions about reality. Like *Repentance*, it takes the form of a recollection based on the personal memory of a narrator figure. The film is set in 1934/35, interpreting this last moment in history when it was still possible genuinely to believe in the ideals of the Revolution and their implementation in Soviet Russia. It is, in German's view, a tribute to those who believed in a myth and perished with it, rather in the same way that Mikhalkov's film is a tribute to those who believed for too long in the ideals of the Revolution and were scorched by its flame. In German's film, the Kirov portraits are gradually replaced by portraits of Stalin, one suspended on a steel car at the end of the film, indicating the change in the political leadership. Lapshin acts through a similarly genuine belief to serve the system as Kotov does, but there is one essential difference:

Lapshin lives in 1934, Kotov in 1936. Although the show trials were still to come, Kirov had, at that point, already been murdered. For the Leningrad-born German, the faults of the system were already apparent, whereas Mikhalkov's character is still able to believe in Stalin's justice in the summer of 1936.

German's realism lies in his portrayal of the harsh life in a communal flat where Lapshin lives, in the routine of his work, in his belief in doing the right thing and sacrificing comfort and personal happiness for the construction of that future about which Kotov (comfortably cushioned) ponders as he drifts in a boat on the river. Mikhalkov's film is set in a completely different world: that of the intelligentsia, whose rich bourgeois cultural heritage and interest in the classical arts had survived well into the 1930s. Far from idealizing, though, Mikhalkov explores the incongruence between two lifestyles, whilst German dwells on the asceticism and poverty of those who devoted their lives to the Revolutionary cause. German depicts all the characters in his film with love, laying the blame at nobody's feet; Mikhalkov renders Kotov's death in a brutal way, taking him violently out of his happy life, while Mitia's death is a tragic but logical conclusion to an existence devoid of meaning. Thus Mikhalkov tilts his sympathies slightly towards the strong, powerful and energetic figure of Kotov.

Stalin after the collapse of the empire

For the film-makers of the 1990s the Stalin era remains a theme of interest, while the emphasis is shifted to issues of culture rather than responsibility and memory that predominate in Abuladze's and German's films. Often, as the two examples discussed here illustrate, they concern themselves with parodic references to Stalinist culture, turning history into a plaything, an artefact, a construct that has little to do with the characters in the film. Artistically, they deny politics the right to play a serious part in their films.

Ivan Dykhovichny's *Moscow Parade* [Prorva, 1992] exposes the immoral sexuality that underlies Stalinist culture. The film juxtaposes a fictional plot with documentary material in order to comment on the nature of high Stalinist culture: the disciplined parades, monumental buildings and muscle-controlled bodies are contrasted with the decadent lifestyle of the heroine Anna (played by the German musical star Ute Lemper). The central character of the film, Sasha, is in charge of a parade in which Stalin's favourite horse is to appear; yet the male horse is frightened by the music and replaced by a female horse with a dildo.

Sasha is impotent, whilst his wife Anna is sexually attractive. She is raped by a secret service agent. Later she finds satisfaction for her sexual energy only with the muscular railway worker Gosha. Sasha loves Anna, just as much as another subsidiary character, a threatened writer-poet, loves a ballerina, but none of these relationships works. Decadence reigns behind the neat and tidy façades and parades of Stalinist culture. Dykhovichny portrays Stalinist culture as a grand carnival of life, whereas for Mikhalkov carnival provides the masks for the reality of the Stalin era.

The film explores the typical landmarks of Stalinist architecture: the metro, the All-Union Exhibition (VDNKh), Red Square, the river stations on the Moscow river, and undermines the façade with decadent music and dance in the milieus of the main characters. The film is less concerned with politics, with individual responsibility or history, than with decadence and culture, with the breakdown of morality in a world where only appearances matter, and with the sexual perversity of all aspects of life, almost in analogy with the political perversion. The threats to individuals, such as the writer, are secondary to the plot; they appear under the surface of the main narrative, just as they occurred under the surface in the reality of the 1930s.

Sergei Livnev's *Hammer and Sickle* [Serp i molot, 1993] parodies and mocks the myth-making of socialist realism and, at the same time, constructs a new myth of the Stalinist past. The film is about a state command in 1936 that the country should have more soldiers. Stalin's aide Ambrosius masterminds an experiment whereby the female tractor-driver Evdokiya Kuznetsova becomes the male construction worker Evdokim Kuznetsov. Evdokim turns out to be a successful model worker in the metro construction brigade, while Ambrosius commits suicide when a change in policy leads to a condemnation of gender transformation since it 'blurs what Soviet men and women are'. The hero Evdokim is awarded a medal, and married to Liza Voronina, a model kolkhoz worker. They literally become models for Vera Mukhina's statue, 'the Worker and the Collective Farm Girl', and a model Soviet family: they adopt a girl, Dolores, who has been orphaned during the Spanish Civil War. One day, Evdokim meets

Vera, who had been his first love as a man. Although Vera wants to remain loyal to her dead husband, they consummate their love; Vera later commits suicide. Evdokim meets Stalin, and as he challenges the Leader's control of his life, he attacks Stalin and is shot. Paralysed and unable to speak, Evdokim is turned into a hero once more: he has supposedly saved Stalin's life and is exhibited as a museum piece. His wife controls his mind (she writes his book *Hammer and Sickle*) and she is also the master of his body, which she uses to satisfy her lust.

If in *Burnt by the Sun* history is an amalgam of personal choices and individual memories, *Hammer and Sickle* challenges the assumption that the individual carries any responsibility for history: history is an artificial construct. Characters are entirely contrived and deprived of choice. Liza and Evdokim are artefacts, creations of a system, the model worker and peasant. Evdokim cannot control his life, which must be devoted to the social good. Liza has no choice either, but her revolt does not go beyond verbal dissent. As artefacts, Liza and Evdokim are types. Ideally, all human beings will end like Evdokim in a museum, displayed to foreign visitors and pioneers as objects who will not change. On one level, Livnev goes further than Mikhalkov – Mitia has no identity, but wears only masks – when he creates a living monument with the paralysed Kuznetsov in a museum, resembling Lenin in the mausoleum and comfortably cushioned on a bed decorated with a hammer and sickle, reduced to total passivity and functioning as a mouthpiece for the state view.

At the same time, Evdokim is a monument that has become alive. Livnev first 'creates' the man Evdokim Kuznetsov in a scientific experiment. Then he creates the spiritual substance for this scientific object – the Socialist worker presented in a documentary that in turn is used to frame stills for the (real) statue of the worker and the farm girl created by Vera Mukhina for the world exhibition in Paris. The artist frames her model from the first black-and-white documentary, while the objects and models watch their creation (and immortalization) in a second documentary that also expands their family and brings to them the orphan Dolores, who suddenly appears – as if from the documentary – among them, amid the reality in which they watch the movie in a viewing room. Dolores too has come alive from a documentary and is artificial. Both Liza and Dolores seem to have been created from film reels. Evdokim (Adam) is created physically by Stalin (God) and his assistants, while the woman (created from Adam's rib) is an offspring and only originates on the second (spiritual/artistic) level of creation, but not on the primary (scientific) one.

The theme of the disparity between creation and reality informs the dialogue: the phrase 'make a fairy tale come true' is repeated several times. The scene between Stalin and Evdokim begins and concludes with an episode from a Chaplin film that the dictator is watching as Evdokim enters; as the film ends, Evdokim is shot – his life is a filmic reality only. Similarly, the statue mocks reality. The 'real' figures are flawed, while the statue remains perfect. The statue functions as a mirror that shows (like the portrait in Wilde's *The Picture of Dorian Gray*) an unchanged face, an ideal, heroic character while Evdokim has betrayed his wife and the ideals of socialism by indulging in his personal feelings for Vera. Indeed, the theme of the soul sold to the devil recurs in the conversation between Stalin and Evdokim. Evdokim is Stalin's product (Stalin as the artist, as God), who made him from the hysterical girl Evdokiya; consenting to the operation, Evdokiya sold her soul to the devil (Stalin). An artefact, Evdokim is seemingly immortal, and even after Dolores, dressed as a Young Pioneer boy, misfires a shot in the museum, it is not clear whether he is dying with a smile of relief and triumph on his face, that he is at last able to act (die), or whether he is immortal.

The reality of documentary films, and also of fairy tales, is – as in *Burnt by the Sun* – more real than reality itself. Mitia tells a fairy tale that Nadia adapts to Soviet realia, and personal history informs the tale of Yatim and Yasum. For Mikhalkov, children understand the level of reality hidden beneath the surface of fairy tales: Nadia says to Kotov that she would be Yadan in the story; children have no imaginary world of their own, but share Soviet reality with adults. Livnev uses historical fact for the tale Liza tells Dolores, mocking history by relating it in the form of a nursery rhyme, and parodying the Sovietization of children's literature. Children are the victims of a blurring between fairy tale and history, between reality and invention. Fairy tales, like art, embellish history, distort it, and transform it into myths.

The theme of the absence of love is another common factor of the two films. For Vera, love transcends death, and she commits suicide when she has betrayed her dead husband. For Evdokim love is merely physical, as it is for Liza, another new Soviet character; their understanding of love is undermined and mocked, when Liza makes love to

Evdokim's paralysed and feelingless body. Evdokim is torn between his memory of the rape (as a woman), which appears in flashbacks, and the night spent with Vera, which appears in a flashback as he is 'raped' by his wife. In scenes of physical love there is always a bitter memory of force (rape), except in the relationship between Vera and Evdokim.

Hammer and Sickle creates a myth, rather than history. Livnev resists the movement of eradicating Soviet symbolism from the map (the change of place names), and erects again the monument of the Worker and the Farm Girl, yet he desacralizes the past by mocking totalitarian values. By making the statue come alive, he freezes life in reality. 'History in these films is known to be secondary, it is an occasion for an artefact, but not for cognition. It is not historical reality that is being reflected here, but a myth that has absorbed it.'[1]

In this respect Livnev's film belongs totally with the postmodernist movement. For Mikhalkov, history is linear in development and created by individual acts. For Livnev, history is fragmented, captured in documentaries and statues, and thus is a product of creative, artistic imagination in which the artefact man becomes a puppet in Stalin's hands, while the individual is destroyed. Both film-makers see history as construct, one subjective and the other mythical.

Thus some common themes emerge in the treatment of the 1930s in these films. The passivity of the individual, who takes action in the imagination only, who condones the crimes of the past, and who is supple enough to be turned into a model rather than make his own choices; the belief in the system and the shattered illusions when the system turns out to betray them; the decadent lifestyle behind the glorious façade. A common denominator is the concern with choice: how long was it possible to believe in the system without realizing its terror? was there a choice to become a cake-baker, a statue, a police officer, a general, or an NKVD officer?

Mikhalkov and the Past

Burnt by the Sun must also be considered in the context of other films by Mikhalkov. Most important in the discussion of themes from other films is *Unfinished Piece for a Mechanical Piano* (1977), based on the works of Anton Chekhov and capturing the atmosphere of the educated bourgeoisie before the Revolution. Many critics have argued that *Burnt by the Sun* is an extension of *Mechanical Piano* into the 1930s.

In *Mechanical Piano* Sofia Egorovna does not recognize her former lover, Mikhail Vasilievich; the parallel to *Burnt by the Sun*, where Mitia enters in a disguise and is not recognized, cannot be missed. Sofia and Mikhail were once in love, when they were students; then she left for the capital (St Petersburg) and did not return for a long time. He waited for her, then gave up his studies: his life was ruined. Again, we see here an inversion of Mitia-Marusia: Mitia left, not Marusia, and her life was ruined by his absence. When Sofia returns she is married to a man who does not care for others although he is a doctor (compare Marusia married to the 'ogre' of the story) and she suggests to Mikhail that they rekindle their affair. Effectively, she proposes the destruction of both their marriages, although his wife Sasha adores him. He refuses, aware that Sasha would die without him. The theme of lost love that cannot be recaptured resounds in *Burnt by the Sun* from this earlier piece.

It is interesting, though, that Sofia's departure was voluntary whereas Mitia's was not: the times have changed. Both Sofia and Mikhail have married, while Mitia remained a bachelor. Both know they belong to each other, but have married other people. Marusia and Sofia have chosen to compromise; whereas Sofia is prepared to give up her marriage for the sake of the past love, Marusia will not go back: she has made a choice and will stand by it, even though it is clear that she is still in love with Mitia: she is tense, her hands shake, she is embarrassed like a teenager in love.

Although an atmosphere of passivity and inertia broods over *Mechanical Piano*, there is some danger in drawing too many parallels between the two films, one set in the Chekhovian tradition on a grand estate, while the Golovins have to retreat to a simple wooden summer-house.

Another earlier film by Mikhalkov lends itself for comparison in its treatment of history. *At Home among Strangers, a Stranger at Home* (1974) is set during the Civil War. The film tells about the trust that the collective places in Egor to accompany a train with gold to the capital, where money is needed to purchase grain from abroad for the starving population. The train is robbed, and Egor takes it upon himself to prove that he was wronged and to retrieve the gold in a solitary fight against bandits and deserters. Although he acts alone, he is guided by the spirit of the collective (flashbacks to the happy past with his comrades), and by the desire to achieve an improvement of society. Like Kotov, he supports the people, believes in the goals of socialism and their capacity to re-educate even thieves. However, the film is more about the integrity and high moral values that Egor holds and inspires in others, rather than about the politics of socialism.

Mikhalkov's interest, then, as represented in these two films, lies in the atmosphere of the life of the educated gentry before the revolution, as shown both in his evocation of Chekhov in *An Unfinished Piece* and the dacha setting of *Burnt by the Sun*; it also features in *The Barber of Siberia*, set in the Russia of 1885. Thematically his concern is with the honesty and integrity of those people who were fighting for the Revolutionary cause (*At Home among Strangers*), or defending their fatherland (*Barber*), a concern reflected also in the character of Kotov. Here Mikhalkov inclines slightly in favour of Kotov, who believes in ideals, whereas Mitia lives through defeat and thrives on his role as a loser.

Mikhalkov's interest in Russia's past is motivated by his desire to look back at pre-Revolutionary Russia to find moral integrity (*Barber*), dwelling on Russia's special role and her need to define her identity without external influences. He wishes to restore the forgotten past of Russia's history in the personal memory of the people. In *Burnt by the Sun* he makes it possible for the individual to accept the past rather than reject those terrible years of terror and the purges, which are often wiped from official history as if there had been neither life nor love in the 1930s.

Note

1   Elena Stishova, 'Razryv', *Iskusstvo kino* 1 (1995), p. 47.

5. The Film in the Mirror of the Press

From Script to Film

The period between inception and realization for *Burnt by the Sun* was extremely short. Mikhalkov discussed the idea for the film in the summer of 1993 with his co-author Rustam Ibragimbekov, and they began to write the script immediately in a dacha in Nizhnii Novgorod. Mikhalkov gained the support of the governor of Nizhnii Novgorod, Boris Nemtsov, and decided to begin shooting immediately, although the film had, as of then, no budget. Mikhalkov has explained this by not wanting to let another year elapse during which his daughter Nadia would have outgrown the phase when he saw her best fit to play her part in the film. Filming lasted from 19 July to 17 November 1993, with the final sequences to be filmed in Moscow. Since the summer of 1993 was rather murky and rainy, and autumn set in earlier than usual, 150,000 leaves had to be stuck on trees for some shots in the village.[1] Editing was completed just in time for the film to be shown at the International Film Festival in Cannes in May 1994, less than a year after production had begun.

The film was made with a $3.6 million budget; it was co-produced by Mikhalkov's studio TriTe (Moscow) and Michel Seydoux's Camera One (Paris), with support from Roskomkino (Russian State Department for Cinematography), the Russian Club of Nizhnii Novgorod, and Camera + (France). After the Festival release in Cannes, *Burnt by the Sun* was premiered in Nizhnii Novgorod on 12 July 1994; the Moscow premiere took place on 2 November 1994.

Mikhalkov and TriTe managed the Russian distribution of the film themselves, rather than contracting a distributor. They had to claim a high rental charge from cinemas to recoup production costs, and therefore they encouraged regional administrations to find sponsors, so that cinemas could pay the rental charge for the film without raising ticket prices. Another condition of the lease was that no illegal video copies would be made to avoid financial loss through the sale of pirated copies.[2]

In the Shadow of the Golden Palm

Burnt by the Sun was premiered in the competition programme of the International Film Festival in Cannes in May 1994, where it was awarded the Grand Prix of the Jury, the second most important award after the Palme d'Or, which went to Quentin Tarantino's *Pulp Fiction*. The first scandal had begun: the Russian press reported the failure of the film to win the main award and, instead of praising how well a Russian film had done – at long last – at an international festival, they shouted 'defeat'. Further rumours followed that Mikhalkov would never participate in the Cannes Film Festival again; such rumours were proved false by the European premiere of *The Barber of Siberia* at the Cannes Festival in 1999.

The first reviews of *Burnt by the Sun* from Cannes came from journalists who had failed to attend the screening.[3] Defeat for all those who had shouted 'defeat' followed when Mikhalkov went on to win the Academy Award (Oscar) in 1995, the third Oscar award won by a Russian film (after Sergei Bondarchuk's *War and Peace* [Voina i mir, 1968] and Vladimir Menshov's *Moscow Does not Believe in Tears* [Moskva slezam ne verit, 1980). In November 1995 the film was nominated for the Russian Film Academy's NIKA award for 1994; Mikhalkov withdrew the film from the list of nominations, since the awards (for 1994) were to be decided in December 1995, thus after *Burnt by the Sun* had received major international awards. On the one hand, Mikhalkov wanted to avoid sweeping the board of the NIKAs; on the other, he wanted to express his dissatisfaction with the delay with which the NIKAs were awarded, saying that it was 'too late' for the film to be decorated with yet another award.[4] The problem of the delay in the awarding of the NIKA was subsequently addressed; the regulations were changed, and in 1998 the ceremony for 1997 films was held in April rather than December. However, Mikhalkov was in for another attack from the press, which now accused him of shunning Russian awards.

The reviews in the Russian press in late 1994 and 1995 were largely neutral, praising a film that had by then received major international acclaim and fared better than any other Russian film. Most critics elaborated on the Chekhovian theme, regarding *Burnt by the Sun* as a continuation of *Unfinished Piece for a Mechanical Piano* in transposing the Chekhovian characters of the earlier film into the 1930s. Others engaged in a search for sources, identifying Gaidar's short story *The Blue Cup* [Golubaia chashka] and Bunin's story *Sunstroke* [Solnechnyi udar, 1925], while many critics debated the issue of the film-maker's condemnation or non-condemnation of revolutionary force and the inertia of the intelligentsia.

Mikhalkov had thus manoeuvred himself into critical cross-fire with this film, as with many others before. The critic Tatiana Moskvina has assessed the critical response to *Burnt by the Sun* in an extremely perceptive, polemical review in the Petersburg cinema journal *Seance*: 'As for Mikhalkov the Russian mass audience, unlike the Russian intelligentsia, has long made its choice. Mikhalkov's film has caused a fairly lively critical debate, which in our country is traditionally indifferent to the taste of the mass audience and which traditionally reflects the view of the intelligentsia.' She suggests that Mikhalkov was expected 'not to show off in Europe and harvest awards, but to repent before the progressive intelligentsia'.[5]

Moskvina identifies five categories of film critics: the embarrassed novelists, secret scriptwriters and directors; the art-politicians who see art as a fight for power and influence; the 'organic' or professional film critics; the 'marginals' who write unprofessionally; and those who write for the tabloid press. Of these, only the first and third groups demonstrate perceptiveness in reviewing *Burnt by the Sun*. It may be appropriate here to introduce another division into the critical response to Mikhalkov's most recent films: the liberal, progressive critics of left-wing newspapers react on the whole with more hostility than, say, those writing for the professional film magazines such as *Premiere*, *Film Art* [Iskusstvo kino] and *Seance*. In any case, both these groups argue their case on the basis of the film rather than engaging in a polemical paraphrase designed only to reduce a work of art to a political statement. Negative comments can be found amongst the formerly dissident intelligentsia, who still believe that art is designed to be understood only by the selected few, but not by wider audiences, not to mention even the 'masses'. Indeed, as is evident from the comment of Igor Vinogradov, cited below, only a film that cannot be understood by the Western viewer is a good Russian film. If that is the rule, then *Burnt by the Sun* is a bad Russian film since the film on the whole can be understood by any viewer. Yet I would contend that a film is like a Russian stacking doll: it offers a multiplicity of layers for interpretation, and the more the patient viewer knows of the culture, the more layers s/he will discover.

Reviews and Rhetoric

The following two reviews, translated here almost in their entirety, reflect the spectrum of Russian film criticism at the top level of the profession. The first is a positive review by the film critic Alexander Kulish, editor-in-chief of the Russian edition of *Premiere*, published in the *Independent Gazette* [Nezavisimaia gazeta]; the second is a review by the postmodernist cultural theorist Viacheslav Kuritsyn published in the newspaper *Today* [Segodnia].

Alexander Kulish 'Endgame' [Konets igry], *Nezavisimaia gazeta*, 9 November 1994

Unexpectedly in our impoverished Russian cinema landscape, a film has appeared that has the potential to please everybody. Nikita Mikhalkov's *Burnt by the Sun* is a real miracle of political and aesthetic correctness, both of which are qualities that no other contemporary Russian film-maker can boast of. It is a film that avoids any hint of extremism in its portrayal of history (it is about the year 1936), and that excludes the influence of contemporary cinematographic fashion, speaking instead in a universal language and resisting any classification as being specifically 'elitist' or 'mass' art.

In *Burnt by the Sun* Mikhalkov removes political judgments from the framework of his film narrative and is interested only in moral and human values instead. Many post-perestroika years have had to pass before such a level of understanding of the epoch could be reached.

What is of interest here is not the clichéd, and therefore meaningless, philosophy of executioner and victim, which is a commonplace in discussions about totalitarianism. Nor is there any of that pathological horror manifest in so many Russian films about the 1930s. With *Burnt by the Sun* the author says farewell to a whole range of films that in essence are political attacks on Stalinism rather than serious works of art. It would be an act of unseemly naiveté to make such films after Mikhalkov's achievement. Therefore the film is not only important for Mikhalkov, who is in top creative form; it also sets a new standard for Russian cinema as a whole. [...]

The director catches precisely the playful element, the carnival atmosphere of the Stalin era. Everybody sings, dances and dresses up in various costumes. Oleg Menshikov's character, the NKVD agent Mitia (cover name 'Pianist') arrives at commander Kotov's (Nikita Mikhalkov) dacha to prepare his arrest. The other agents of this secret organization are introduced as members of a philharmonic orchestra. Among the large number of dacha inhabitants are a former conductor and a former opera singer. The action takes place on the Day of Dirigibles, and the entire village is getting ready for this holiday.

The impression is created that all the characters of the film are taking part in a grandiose communal game. They play sincerely at the construction of the 'bright tomorrow' according to the rules of emotional experience. And all these absurd war games in the collective farm fields, the game of the gas attack that disrupts the relaxation of peaceful citizens at the beach, and the construction of the completely absurd and outsized dirigible bearing Stalin's portrait – all these are steps that are gradually leading everybody into the communist future. The main thing is to comply with the rules of the game.

Commander Kotov, a legendary revolutionary and Stalin's friend, is one of those who devised the game. The 'pianist' Mitia, on the other hand, has robbed the game of its innocence and its purely aesthetic charm.

Some time ago, Kotov casually destroyed Mitia's personal life and, taking advantage of his high rank, married Mitia's fiancée. Now, after many years of working as a spy in Paris, the 'pianist' returns to take revenge. [...]

Burnt by the Sun records the moment when illusions are destroyed. The catastrophe for everybody sets in when the rules of the game are no longer observed, when one's inner life no longer equals the outer life, and when no change of clothes can be of assistance. Therefore, the false 'players' of the philharmonic orchestra can strike the real commander in the face. But another game begins here, which belongs to the sphere behind the looking glass.

This is a nice, beautiful and cheerful film with a sad and bloody ending. There is no space here to describe the film, scene by scene, in order to demonstrate the supreme mastery displayed by Nikita Mikhalkov. [...] Mikhalkov's film can, without exaggeration, be regarded as Event Number One in our current film season. It can be rivalled only by other films by Nikita Mikhalkov, who in recent years has been extremely productive.

Viacheslav Kuritysn, 'The Reel's Territory' [Territoriia chasti], *Segodnia*, 27 October 1994.

It seems to me worthwhile to specify the context in the broadest sense. So broad that it begins to become diffuse, but maybe the desire or non-desire to catch up with context is today our number one problem. This film belongs to a certain type of contemporary cultural consciousness: the type that gives rise to the prose of Sorokin and the poetry of Kibirov. In the cinema we have *Moscow Parade*, and perhaps *Hammer and Sickle*, and some works that made less of a stir. [...] I am talking about a rather contemporary attitude to 'socialist realism' and the reality that stands (or lies) behind it (although according to many, quite convincing, theories, socialist realism is characterized by the fact that it was at that time this reality itself). At the beginning (I have already written about this, but there's no harm in repeating myself) there was the communist, socialist attitude, in the course of which children were named Dub (Give improved concrete! [Daesh' uluchshennyi beton!]), Dazdraperm (Long Live May the First! [Da zdravstvuet pervoe maia!]), and Uriurvkos (Hurray! Yuri's in space! [Ura, Yura v kosmose!]). In its place came the anti-Soviet, freedom-loving attitude; the dissidents called their offspring quite differently: Aisolnas (Alexander Isaevich Solzhenitsyn is free [Aleksandr Isaevich Solzhenitsyn na svobode]). The third attitude: socialist realism is a unique aesthetic system, capable of producing the most fairy-tale-like effects, the most unexpected fates and characters, and very organic subject-matter. For instance, the conflict between good and better, which on the lips of sarcastic Soviet critics becomes as commonplace as the joke about the names – a bogeyman – may be considered purely on an aesthetic level, as a type of history that is simply characteristic of such a system. But

Mikhalkov's gesture is an inversion. A reprogramming of this conflict to one between 'bad' and 'worse'.

It is clear that Nikita Mikhalkov's self-consciousness differs from the consciousness of skittish sots-art;[6] he is worried not by the reflective steps along which socialist realism descends into postmodernism. [...] He is worried about Man. An attitude 'from here' towards the people 'from there'. In press conferences he explains that he did not defend Commander Kotov, but the life that flowed then and still flows now. Then, too, people fell in love, kissed, and drank tea. Everything is clear, all too clear.

Artistic logic is, of course, not the same thing as moral-ethical logic. The method of 'defending' life and people is the same: to tell of their lives without putting them in our own understanding of the epoch, like a fly into some jam. This is what somewhat irritates one in the film: its claim to globality. Chekhovian concepts underscore the contrast of the seasons, the changes in the people's fates, the transformation of the characters, the contrast of then and now, – in short, literary concepts. The relationship with 1936 is thoroughly principled: it is not surprising when, at the end, the NKVD men strike Mikhalkov's hero in the face at inordinate length, thereby confirming one's growing impression that the film could – just could – have been much shorter. Almost the most important thing, the atmosphere around the film: Mikhalkov's statement that the non-victory in Cannes is no more and no less than a defeat for Russia. Quite remarkably, tons of pathos are involved, but Mikhalkov is such a good director that he makes these tons melt away and disperse as though they had never been. And what remains is a wonderful story about love and the fireball, unique in the fact that it could have happened this way only in Russia in the 1930s, and it is additionally dear because it is contaminated with the meaning of some local literary classic (that degree of national hermetism that is interpreted by world audiences as natural physiognomy and not as patriotic excess or exoticism). Ideal cinema.

Ideal even more since it provokes the observer into expressions of this sort: it is nothing special, and yet it is very good. 'It makes no original contribution to Russian culture, aesthetics, philosophy, history' (Gladilshchikov), but the film is nevertheless remarkable (Gladilshchikov). It really is nothing special, but there are, at the same time, some essentials: the Kremlin, somebody marching, the practice of the gas attack, admittedly, taken from *The Golden Calf*, the anxious scene between Father and Daughter (which M. Andreev traces to *The Blue Cup*), and finally the blue cup itself, and various other cups, and the soup bowl on the tablecloth, and the wicker chairs (of course, *Burnt by the Sun* is also an 'urga', the sacred territory of love into which people intrude).[7] And the altogether soapy titles: this and that befell the characters some time later. And the classic move: the character who gets under everybody's feet and who has an absurd function, the man on the truck driving around the neighbouring fields in search of the village of Zagorianka. Everything is very ordinary, no tricks from the cameraman, no cover-ups, emphatically simple cinema. Life is shown. Half of the dialogue is accidental, insignificant utterances spoken away from the microphone: what does it matter what they mutter in their life at the dacha?

Mikhalkov manages to shoot great cinema with non-cinematic, theatrical acting. Mikhalkov and Menshikov emphatically act, they act so well and almost desperately that this too may be seen as a sort of move by Russia against non-Russia: as the move of the Russian, 'Stanislavskian' tradition against the emphatically cinematic western stylization where the actor is a 'model actor' (*naturshchik*), a puppet, a cinegenic something, playing not from within, but played upon from without. [...] The third peak of the triangle is Ingeborga Dapkunaite, who emphatically exposes the texture without worrying too much about the balance between intention and gesture: the gesture is coloured, reflected in the faces of Menshikov and Mikhalkov. This is a very interesting arrangement: in the given context the female member of the triangle is associated with Russia. And Mikhalkov the director – we have to assume, unconsciously – allies himself to a well-known idea, according to which Russianness, receptive femininity, and passivity all appear as synonyms. This partly explains the pathos, and also some 'ambiguous' social-political steps of the illustrious filmmaker.

But may the artist always triumph over the thinker: this bright optimism makes it possible to identify some demonic themes in *Burnt by the Sun*. Let us assume that before us we have a languid, aesthetic, almost decadent film about the tragedy of an artist. Menshikov's character, a musician, is as talented as Menshikov himself. Apart from talent, God has given him earthly love (house, wood, field, veranda, jam). A certain commander 'has taken everything away'. Mitia returns to arrest this same commander. To what extent all his exercises are mere revenge is a debatable question. But if it is vengeance, then not against Commander Kotov. Because it was not Commander Kotov who took away his music, and nor was it simply the communist system: the system put itself in a demonic and supernatural position, leading into scarcely human territory, and Mitia suffered directly from a global fate. He lost what Kotov could not have taken from him: more than a pathetic Red hero could have done – he took away his Talent. Mitia feels that he has suffered at the hand of some Absolute (in the most concrete version – from global Evil). He takes his revenge not on Kotov, but on the entire nest: and two days later Marusia and Nadia find out why he had come. He plays with them like a cat with a cockroach, as a musician plays his note. He takes out his revenge on the visible world: his capacity for seemingly comfortable organization, his apparent authenticity, his naive belief in logic, justice, good. With all this – earthly things – he knows how to behave best of all.

If we are to mention Chekhov: in Chekhov's story 'Visiting Friends' a lawyer comes to the dacha of some old friends and they annoy him by their inability to handle things. [...] Just as Mitia produces a sweet from under the ceiling, which he had hidden ten years ago. None of those in the room could ever do that, and Mitia has good reason to despise these people: they believe in that life that tiptoes before him. He knows *everything*, but there are, it appears, forces stronger than he is. Non-life is larger. His disdain for life is an attempt to stand next to that non-life. Yes, he stands to attention before the portrait of Stalin that drifts behind the dirigible, but there is a frame in which he and the portrait are the same size, one against the background of the other. Similarly Kotov, who has a photo of himself with Stalin, erroneously believed that he and Stalin were of equal magnitude. What is the meaning of two living people on a faded photo? Quite different is the Artist, emerging into the field, and the huge portrait of the dictator under an air bubble. That is scale.

And the truckdriver who is shot like a dog and who never reaches his Zagorianka: what does he know about the world? This is boring. The wind carries the leaves away, which rustle under the Poet's feet. And Russian roulette, one cartridge in the drum, a game for every evening: what will become of his temple? Such is service in the NKVD, *sic gloria mundi*. What can possibly depend on you? Boring. Some fireball. Boring.

Tra-ta-ta. Gentle farewell to the sea. Tra-ta.

Dissonant Voices

Many of those who have written about the film have strong views and feelings, either positive or negative. Kuzminsky's remarks reflect the most abusive tone used when discussing the film, whilst his comments lack professionalism and provide no analysis. Larisa Miller offers a reader's response to the film, finding in it parallels with contemporary Russia. Boris Liubimov is a renowned theatre and arts critic, who comments here very perceptively on the 'positive' events and achievements of the year 1936 that is historically associated with Terror; he dwells on personal happiness and love that pervaded even the most atrocious historical epochs. The two thinkers Igor Vinogradov and Vladimir Novikov express very well the intelligentsia's view that art cannot be for the masses; on these grounds, they personally dislike the film. Finally, Mark Kushnirovich's response represents a simplified, allegorical reading of the film.

Boris Kuzminsky, *Segodnia*, 24 October 1995
Suicidal exhibitionism, fantastic, bestial candour of despair. As a spectator I am utterly indifferent to the social orientation of the director who made this inarticulate, excruciating masterpiece. [...] It turns out that the character of Oleg Menshikov is a mocking parody of the intellectual and creative elite, of the people's conscience. The heroine played by Ingeborga Dapkunaite is an allegory of Russia, sluggishly serving Stalin's satrap. The episodes with Avangard Leontiev are an unpardonable manifestation of anti-Semitism. It turns out that this film spits in the face of all of us, and that means mine as well. A totalitarian agit-prop, denser than *A Slave of Love*, a piece of 'mass-culture' more than *Kinfolk* with its primitivism. A Russian stacking doll for export with more fat content than *Urga*.

Larisa Miller, 'Such a cinema' [Takoe vot kino'] *Ekran i stsena* 6 (1995), p. 2
The film *Burnt by the Sun* is not only about the past but also about the present. The tanks that roar and rumble at the beginning of the film continue to roar and rumble in the present. Now as well people rush about between metal and smoke, be it in Moscow or in Grozny. Half a century has passed since that summer's day that the film narrates, but the nonsense still goes on. [...] There is no idyll in Russia, and there

never has been. But, strangely enough, there were and are happy people.

Boris Liubimov, 'The Sun of the Dead' [Solntse mertvykh], *Segodnia*, 22 November 1994

The Year 1936. The year when the great ballerina Semenova is on tour in Paris. When Aleinikov plays in the film *The Brave Seven*, well, no worse than his Hollywood counterparts. When in Moscow alone four of the world's greatest directors are still alive, and when there are so many outstanding actors that they have to accept supporting roles. When three of the world's greatest poets – Akhmatova, Pasternak and Mandelstam – live in a 'nameless country'. And in this same year 1936, Akhmatova writes two classic poems, published only in 1940, dedicated to two other geniuses, and when Pasternak writes (and publishes!) two cycles, 'The Artist' and 'Travel Notes'. Bulgakov's *Molière* was performed only seven times at the Arts Theatre: what is surprising is not that it was banned, but that it was staged at all. And which play written in that same year in the free West is greater than Bulgakov's? It is not just that a country shaken by twenty years of terror was so rich in people, or that cinema and theatre, ballet and opera, literature and science, philology, philosophy, and theology were not destroyed completely. Life is indestructible: in 1937 Akhmadulina and Petrushevskaya were born, Rasputin and Vampilov, Averintsev and Panchenko, Bitov and Mikhalkov-Konchalovsky (a theme that perhaps is of some interest to the author of the film) – probably because their parents loved one another in the summer and autumn of 1936, and even in the winter of 1937. 'The children of Russia's terrible years...' were born out of a love that could not be destroyed.

'Is Soviet Culture Nonsense?' [Sovetskaia kul'tura – nonsens?] Igor Vinogradov and Vladimir Novikov in discussion with Natalia Sirivlia, *Iskusstvo kino*, 4 (1996), pp. 44–51 (48–49)

Vladimir Novikov: 'Unwatchability' reigns in our cinema. I had great difficulty sitting through the film *Burnt by the Sun*, which has been laden with an Oscar and other prestigious awards [...] Although I have not yet changed my opinion of the film, I have begun to think: maybe Nikita Mikhalkov has performed here some turn toward the middle-brow belles-lettres that ought to occupy an essential part of the cultural spectrum? After all, not without reason did Dostoevsky call himself a man of belles-lettres, and so did Turgenev. It seems to me that high art develops not against the current of belles-lettres, but, as it were, on its base. Mikhalkov, I suppose, is no genius as a director. He is not one of those who discovers absolutely new paths. He lacks the genius of Tarkovsky or Kira Muratova, who are visionaries. He is a good craftsman, a master of high-quality psychological cinema. . . .

Igor Vinogradov: The view of a foreign intellectual who has not really lived our life and who does not feel on his own skin the false notes, the fabrication, and the speculation manifested in *Burnt by the Sun*, his view paradoxically coincides with the view of the average Russian spectator. In the West they want to see Russia like that: melodramatically simplified, understandable, without insoluble existential problems. And the native Russian philistine wants to see our past in roughly the same mythological mist: look, what strong and healthy fellows our Russian commanders were, and what have they done with them? And those people were all from the intelligentsia, that White Guard scum. [. . .] *Burnt by the Sun* is a well thought-out film, but particularly ideological, made to suit both 'them and us'.

Mark Kushnirovich, 'Tale about the Stupid Mouse Named Kotov' [Skazka o glupom myshonke po imeni Kotov], *Literaturnaia gazeta*, 14 December 1994

To use the childish, allegorical language that the heroes of the film love so much: it is simply a game of cat and mouse. First the commander was the cat. Then Mitia became the cat. Then they went too far in their game, as children do, and began to break the rules, and even became slightly confused about who was who. But the real tomcat, the one with the whiskers, was not far away. He saw everything, knew everything, and grinned slyly into his feline whiskers. And then he got up, stretched, and . . . rose above the earth. Like the sun. It is to him that the film-makers point in the final episodes of the film. He is the secret launcher of the fireballs. He is the Sun who burns the heroes in their death agony.

Professional critics

Finally, some responses by critics writing for professional film journals.

The first critic, Andrei Plakhov, is an internationally renowned film critic who has been a member of several FIPRESCI juries.

Andrei Plakhov, 'Mikhalkov against Mikhalkov' [Mikhalkov protiv Mikhalkova] *Seans* 9 (1994), p. 21

For Mikhalkov's oeuvre *Burnt by the Sun* truly sets a model, a standard [...] The tangle of love, jealousy and betrayal set against the backdrop of the idyllic dacha landscape in '36 is dashingly unravelled by Mikhalkov and his co-author Rustam Ibragimbekov. According to the latter, the subject-matter is not opportunistic, and the film could, in theory, have been made ten years ago. Indeed, from the viewpoint of form *Burnt by the Sun* follows the traditions of the 'cinema of the Brezhnev era with a mark of quality'. The intimate psychologism and the picturesque beauty of the first half change in the second part to a revival of the grand epic style, which has gone with the wind of history and evokes nostalgic pain. As for the content, it is indeed our 'Gone with the Wind', a conservative film-novel with a love intrigue, projected onto the backdrop of history. [...] When we listen to Kotov's words about why revolution and communism are necessary (so that everyone would have soft heels) you do not think what a good father Mikhalkov is, but how hard it is to make a fairy tale come true. And the more beautiful the fairy tale, the harder it gets.

Dmitri Bykov, 'Burnt by the Wind, or Gone with the Sun' [Utomlennye vetrom, ili Gone with the sun] *Literaturnaia gazeta*, 14 December 1994

The anti-intelligentsia mood is gaining strength at present for a good reason. The intelligentsia has for a long time (ever since its formation) brought down upon itself cataclysms during which it has lost everything it possibly could. [...] They're good at talking, masters of nostalgia, but they have not evolved a truly chivalrous code of honour – in which they would adhere to blatantly unpopular viewpoints, fulfil their duty and defend themselves to the bitter end. That is why Mitia's suicide at the end does not create the explosion of compassion and protest that overwhelms every normal spectator during the brutal beating of Kotov.

Alexander Arkhangelsky, 'Mikhalkov's Right Hand and Left Hand' [Desnitsa i shuitsa N.S. Mikhalkova], *Iskusstvo kino*, 3 (1995), pp. 5-8

The old people at the dacha in *Burnt by the Sun* are like the heroes of *Mechanical Piano* who have aged and survived into the 1930s. They have wept their lives away, missed their opportunities, learnt nothing, and now they sleep off their rabbit's sweet dreams inside a wolf's belly. [...] The commander has taken from life what he wanted to take, according to the law of the stronger. Yes, he shed much blood, but – let us note – in an honest fight. Admittedly, he intruded into Mitia's life, settled in his house, appropriated his love, but, my friends, he took her because Mitia could not or did not wish to defend his love. Kotov does not seek revenge, he is too powerful for that, and therefore he is condescending towards the 'representatives' of the pre-Soviet Russia that he abolished: he lives with them side-by-side at their dacha, tolerates their old-fashioned escapades, is condescending towards their incomprehension of the new life and their human weaknesses (foreign medicines, their habit of slapping the maid on her plump backside, or their secret drinking).

Mitia is completely different. He has lost, and has not found the courage within himself to acknowledge his defeat. Or at least to die honourably. He has not only agreed to collaborate with the organs of the NKVD, hired by those whom he hates and despises; he has not only permitted himself to turn up at his childhood house to enact there a bloody comedy; he not only avenges himself against the commander, aware of the power of his strength, and therefore relying on the strength of his own power; but – and this is far worse – he takes revenge against Kotov's young daughter Nadia by removing her father. He is villain enough to take revenge on his beloved; and, in the last resort, he avenges himself against Heaven by taking his own life.

Yuri Bogomolov, 'Drown the Traces – and Bring Forth the Complexes. . .' [Kontsy v vodu – kompleksy naruzhu. . .], *Iskusstvo kino*, 3 (1995), pp. 13–18.

One can bisect, quarter, fragment and reassemble the biography of a man just as one can the history of a country (before October, after October; before the war, after the war; before perestroika, after perestroika), but not the heart, the personality. Although, if you try hard enough. . . True, Marusia did not manage to. She made her choice before the stray fireball struck her house and her life: she showed Mitia the door. And Mitia, eventually, will make his choice: he will cut his wrists. Only Sergei Kotov is freed from making a choice, thanks to the protection of his best friend, Comrade Stalin. The commander will not have to execute himself; he will be executed by his comrades from the Party and the Revolution. Also a sort of suicide.

Suicide is one of the most persistent motifs in the film, which begins and ends with a suicide. It is a way of concealing one's guilt. Whereas the less persistent themes of self-deception and self-betrayal (which even Mikhalkov's protagonist Kotov cannot evade) are a means of justifying oneself before the past and the future.

But what seems so clear and obvious on the scale of private life and individual fate is hazy and obscured on the level of history. Some people nowadays want to settle scores with the Soviet times. Some want to get even with the present day. Some want to marry off the two epochs and join them together in a new manner. Viewed from this angle, the allegory that can be read into the film clarifies some questions. The Soviet regime, embodied by commander Sergei Kotov, destroyed old Chekhovian Russia, and on its ruins the Soviet regime married and settled down in the surviving ancestral nests, and started moralizing to the defeated class of the intelligentsia: why were you so bad at defending your Russia? [...]

Both Mitia and Kotov paid with their lives. It would seem that all the traces were buried. But these traces surface again and again. However cunningly Nikita Mikhalkov hides them in his film, they are nevertheless visible. And how much he (and many others) would like to join socialist Russia with the non-socialist Russia of the future – almost in the way that Mikhalkov's once distinguished parents (and not only they) had hoped to combine Bolshevik reality with the pre-Revolutionary education level of the nobility.

The Question of Guilt: Who is to Blame?

The pivotal issue addressed in this film, as in other films about the Stalin era, is the question of responsibility. In a system such as the Soviet one, where the individual was 'freed' from choice, did the individual have any scope for making decisions? In a totalitarian state, does the individual have any choice, and, if so, where does the choice lie (in Mitia's case, die or collaborate)? Ultimately, who is responsible: the system or the individual? Critics have commented a great deal on the issue of choice and guilt in *Burnt by the Sun*, seeking to ascertain whom the film-maker condemns – the Reds or the Whites; the revolutionaries or the intelligentsia; dreamers or thinkers.

Geoffrey Macnab, 'Burnt by the Sun', *Sight and Sound*, 8 (1995), pp. 41–42

Mikhalkov refuses to judge his characters or the system that formed them: he neither waxes nostalgic for some long-lost, pre-Revolutionary Arcadia nor lapses into crude polemic about the 'evils' of the Soviet state, and his film is all the richer for it.

Louis Menashe, 'Burnt by the Sun', *Cineaste* XXI, 4 (1995): 43–44

Mikhalkov's own sympathies as a Russian nationalist and monarchist [. . .] probably lean to Mitia, but his own powerful presence in the film tilts reactions in favour of Kotov.

Evgenia Tirdatova, 'In the Tango Rhythm' [V ritme tango], *Ekran i stsena*, 33–4 (1994), p. 4

Mikhalkov does not condemn anybody. The fatal sin of Mitia's betrayal is washed away by his death, and his tragedy becomes equal to that of the man whom he betrayed. [. . .] But, according to Mikhalkov, life goes on. Children are born, rivers flow, autumn follows summer, and these years, like so many others, must not be erased from the memory of the people. Nobody has the right to do that.

Maksim Andreev, 'The Unconditional Effect of a Falcon's Farewell Cry Struck Down in Mid-Flight by a Fireball' [Bezuslovnyi effekt proshchal'nogo krika sokola, srazhennogo sharovoi molniei na letu], *Segodnia*, 10 August 1994

Evil fights evil. There is no good. [. . .] Everybody is guilty.

Lev Anninsky, 'Scorched by the Sun' [Spalennye solntsem], *Ogonek*, 4 (1995)

Both burn. The commander is shot. The Chekist cuts his wrists. If he had not cut his wrists, then he would have been shot, too, next after the commander, as one witness too many.

Alexander Arkhangelsky, N. S. Mikhalkov's Right Hand and Left Hand [Desnitsa i shuitsa N. S. Mikhalkova], *Iskusstvo kino,* **3 (1995), pp. 5–8**

In *Burnt by the Sun,* judgement is pronounced. From my point of view, it is an absolutely wrong judgement. Mikhalkov, indignant at Mitia's vindictiveness, nevertheless himself takes revenge upon the unsuccessful snivellers who were defeated, and yet survived. I am willing to admit that Mikhalkov's vindictiveness is of a peculiar type, that it is dictated by his ardent zeal for the Russia that they surrendered, that they shamefully handed over to the Kotovs, whom they now have to love, because they, like all true victors, are magnanimous and imposing.

Overall, the response from Russian critics is typical of their attitude to Nikita Mikhalkov: the film has enjoyed great success with audiences both at home and abroad, because it is not made for an elite audience, and therefore it is scathed by the intelligentsia. The same pattern is true for the critical response to *The Barber of Siberia.*

Notes

1 Leonid Vereshchagin, Interview with Yulia Khomiakova, 'Oskar, Nika i Feliks vstrechaiutsia na Malom Kozikhinskom', *KinoGlaz,* 3 (1995), pp. 34–6.
2 Nikita Mikhalkov, 'Rezhisser ne dolzhen dolgo nakhodit'sia pod obaianiem svoei kartiny. Eto opasno', *Iskusstvo kino* 3 (1995), pp. 9–13.
3 The critic Mikhail Trofimenkov, writing in *Smena* (4 July 1994), cited in Tat'iana Moskvina, 'Sud nad pobeditelem', *Seans* 10 (1994), pp. 27–32.
4 Yuri Gladil'shchikov, 'Utomlennye "Nikoi"', *Segodnia,* 28 November 1995.
5 Moskvina, 'Sud nad pobeditelem', pp. 27, 28.
6 sots-art, in analogy to pop-art, parodies the ideological icons of Soviet Marxism.
7 The author is here referring to Ilf and Petrov's satirical novel *The Golden Calf* [Zolotoi telenok, 1931], and to Arkadi Gaidar's children's story *The Blue Cup* [Golubaia chashka, 1936]. His reference to an 'urga' alludes, of course, to Mikhalkov's film of the same title [Urga, 1991].

Conclusion

Burnt by the Sun is, without doubt, the first internationally known film made in Russia after the collapse of the Soviet state and of its film industry.

From the point of view of Mikhalkov's treatment of history the film has, as many critics noted at the time, ended the series of films made about the 1930s that had begun with Abuladze's *Repentance*. The film portrays both the lifestyle, the potential for love, and the hope for the future of the generation of Kotov and Marusia. From the viewpoint of genre Mikhalkov has explored the melodramatic plot of a woman between two men, one strong, active and not verbose, the other weak, passive, and articulate. They also happen to represent different political views, and different social classes. But the choice for Marusia is personal. Consequently, there is no political or class victory to be achieved by either of the 'competitors' for her love; there is only personal loss.

Allegorically speaking, Nadia is a product of the intelligentsia and Bolshevism; as a cross-breed, she has been exiled to Kazakhstan. The parallel here to Mikhalkov's own background (his mother from the aristocracy, his father the court poet of Stalin's Russia) cannot be missed. The new generation is a cross-breed of the new Soviet style and the old Russia, yet it is the product of a love that was destroyed by the system.

For Mikhalkov, there are no winners. Yet what remains ambiguous throughout the film is the film-maker's view of the issue of responsibility for history: for Mikhalkov, neither Kotov (who believes he has a choice), nor Mitia (who believes he has no choice) are in control of their destiny. Ultimately, then, *Burnt by the Sun* is an apologia for action and inaction in a period of terror and tyranny. Mitia's resistance to the cult of Stalin and Kotov's support for the Leader bear the same result: death.

Further Reading

Reviews in English:

David Gillespie and Natal'ia Zhuravkina, 'Nikita Mikhalkov's *Utomlennye solntsem*', *Rusistika* 13 (June 1996), pp. 58–61.

Geoffrey Macnab, 'Burnt by the Sun', *Sight and Sound* 8 (1995), pp. 41–2.

Louis Menashe, 'Burnt by the Sun', *Cineaste* XXI, 4 (1995), pp. 43–4.

Tatiana Moskvina, 'La Grande Illusion', in *Russia on Reels*, Birgit Beumers (ed.), London, 1999, pp. 91–104.

For a full bibliography of Russian publications and reviews see *Kinograf* 4 (1997), pp. 148–165.

Contemporary Russian Film:

Lynne Attwood, (ed.), *Red Women on the Silver Screen: Soviet Women and Cinema from the Beginning to the End of the Communist Era*, London, 1993.

E. Berry and A. Miller-Pogacar (eds), *Re-Entering the Sign*, Ann Arbor, 1995.

Nancy Condee, (ed.), *Soviet Hieroglyphics: Visual Culture in Late Twentieth-century Russia*, Bloomington and London, 1995.

Gregory Freidin, (ed.), *Russian Culture in Transition*, Stanford, 1993.

Andrew Horton and Michael Brashinsky, *The Zero-Hour: Glasnost and Soviet Cinema in Transition*, Princeton, 1991.

C. Kelly and D. Shepherd (eds.) *Russian Cultural Studies: An Introduction*, Oxford, 1998.

Anna Lawton, *Kinoglasnost*, Cambridge, 1992.
D. Shalin, *Russian Culture at the Crossroads*, Boulder (Col.) and Oxford, 1996.

Websites

Database of Russian Films. http://www.agama.com/cinema/
Kirill and Methodius Database. http://www.km.ru/cinema/
Nikita Mikhalkov's website. http://mikhalkov.comstar.ru